The
Filipino
American
Journey

Stories of Survival & Success

By

Josie Moralidad Ziman

Published and printed

by **TATAY JOBO ELIZES.**
Self-Publisher
in 2019,
under the permission and
authorization

of **JOSIE MORALIDAD ZIMAN,**

author and owner of the copyright to this book. The copyright owner can withdraw this permission at her discretion without any objection from Tatay Jobo Elizes at any time. Printing of this book is using the present day method of Print-On-Demand (POD) system, where prints will never run out of copies to be available for posterity. The copyright owner is free to republish with other publishers anytime.

ISBN - 13: 9781726724975

Contacts: job_elizes@yahoo.com +
josieziman701@gmail.com

Websites: http://tinyurl.com/mj76ccq +
www.tatayjoboelizes.webs.com +

oooooo

TABLE OF CONTENTS

1

FIL-AM BEATS CANCER WITH FAITH HOPE AND FAMILY

Edward Logan of Lorton, VA., is a walking, breathing tale of Christmas – a story of hope, charity and yes, miracles.

He's cheated death so many times – a bus accident in the Philippines when he was just six, a stroke he suffered in 2010. But he faced the most serious test yet in 2015 when he said he didn't feel well and checked himself in at the Fair Oaks Inova Hospital in Fairfax, Va. He was later diagnosed to have leukemia.

He was the youngest of four siblings and was fortunate to attend University of the Philippines in Diliman, one of the Philippines' most prestigious learning institutions, on a scholarship at the College of Arts & Letters.

He arrived in the United States in 1995 and was adopted by a retired couple in Sedona, Arizona. "I was introduced to my adopted parents by my biological aunt Remy Logan Nelton. She is the younger sister of my father and married to an American Evangelistic Preacher, Rev. Louie Nelton, a colleague of Rev. Billy Graham.

"My adoptive parents were tireless advocates of helping kids around the world by opening their home to provide them a better life, great education and the blessing to live in America." he recounted to the Manila Mail.

Mr. Logan completed his college education in the U.S. on full scholarships (estimated to be worth over $200,000) for both undergraduate and graduate studies. He earned his diploma on Political Science and

International Affairs at Northern Arizona University, and also graduate degrees from George Washington University. Cornell, Stanford University and Regent University.

He was a 2013 Partners Fellow by the American Council for Technology/Industry Advisory Council. In 2004, he was inducted to the Asian American Hall of Fame and made it to the Who's Who of American Executives and Professionals. He worked as a Senior Executive for CACI International where he helped win multimillion-dollar litigation support services for federal government clients.

"As a member of the senior executive team with the CACI International Litigation Support, I closed and won new business deals worth almost over $1 billion from the FDIC, SEC, DOJ and other agencies," he disclosed.

Everything was turning out so well for the young Fil-Am as he rode the American Dream. He married Sue Yoon, a Korean American who works as an immigration lawyer. They have a 13-year old son Edward and a 10-year old daughter Elyse. Both are very gifted kids and currently enrolled in the Academic Advanced Placement (AAP) program in Fairfax County, Virginia but it all seemed to crash down in 2015. "I was shocked at first when the ER doctor at the Inova Fair Oaks Hospital told me I had cancer," he recalled.

"The ER doctor did not tell me what kind of cancer I had. I was transferred to Inova Fairfax Hospital to run more tests and validate their findings. I was diagnosed with an aggressive precursor B Acute Lymphoblastic leukemia (ALL) also known as blood cancer," he explained.

He said he's thankful his wife stood by him through his ordeal. His faith and positive attitude also placed him a better position to fight the cancer. He underwent intensive chemotherapy and was almost over the first cycle of treatment when he got an infection and his liver started to deteriorate, leading to a new, separate medical crisis - septic infection, respiratory failure, cardiac arrest. He had to be resuscitated on Nov. 5, 2015. He developed pneumonia from the tube that was inserted into him, injuring his larynx. A tracheostomy was done, then a g-tube to deliver a liquid diet directly to his stomach.

Mr. Logan lost 45 pounds. He was moved to a rehabilitation facility but his health remained critical, losing his sense of taste, eyes inflamed and suffering a brain clot, doctors said he badly needed a bone marrow transplant - a procedure that was available for him at the John Hopkins Hospital in Baltimore, Maryland but he needed a donor. It turns out his best bet was an elder brother in the Philippines that he's not seen or talked to for over two decades.

"After the test results came my biological brother was a half match and confirmed to be a potential donor. On this great news, there were factors we have to go through since my brother will need to have a visa issued by the US Embassy in Manila. It was indeed a challenging task, to make our case to the consulate that my brother has the strong ties to return to the Philippines after the medical procedure. I am truly blessed that God answered my prayers and my brother was granted a multiple 10-year visa," he said.

The transplant was successfully completed in October 2016. His latest tests show that he is now 100 percent in remission. Still, he is currently suffering from graft vs. host disease (GVHD) on his eyes, mouth and skin - a side effect caused by his brother's cells attacking his immune system. These are being managed by using various steroids and medications.

When asked by Manila Mail If he ever questioned God about his struggles, especially with his bout with cancer, Mr. Logan says emphatically, "no!" He believes his faith helped him through his battle with cancer.

"Throughout this incredible journey, God has shown me His unconditional love by experiencing wonderful miracles firsthand. I am a firm believer that fear make you think that nothing is possible but I know deep in my heart that through faith in God, all things are possible," he proclaimed. "It is time that I let every person I meet know about God's love, and it is time that every conversation be seasoned with His grace," inspired by his own blessings and miracle this Christmas, he has dedicated himself to helping find a cure for children with cancer of the blood through a non- profit program he's formed named, aptly enough, "Bloodgevity."

2

A RANDOM AIRPORT ENCOUNTER LEADS TO GRANDMAS' LOVE, MARRIAGES

There's "good random" and "bad random", host Conan O'Brien observed, just as there's "good silly" and "bad silly". For Mila Anguluan and Dr. Nancy "Rusty" Barcelo, both grandmothers in their 60s, a serendipitous encounter at the Minneapolis Airport four years ago has led to love and a marriage.

It was Oct. 27, 2014; Mila was 61 and Rusty was 67, both preoccupied with their laptops while waiting for their flights at the Minneapolis Airport lounge when a boy asked Mila if she saw a cane his grandmother left nearby. "I noticed a cane nearby. Rusty said that was hers," Mila recalled, "There was a guitar case beside the cane. I asked her if that was her guitar. She said yes, So began a conversation that's still going on."

Anguluan, born in Cagayan Valley, was on her way home to Honolulu. Rusty, a Mexican-American, was catching a flight back to New Mexico where she helmed a college.

"There was no notion of romance during our first meeting. It was for me, simply feeling good that I have met a person, that we have talked about a lot of things. It never occurred to me that Rusty was a lesbian. She told me about her music and compositions; I talked about the Filipino folksongs that I sang to the Ilocano elders in Hawaii.

"Once we got started, we could not stop talking to each other. She shared story from her childhood that she was writing for her memoirs. It touched me so deeply that I was moved to respond, by spontaneously singing my favorite lullaby, Ugoy ng Duyan. Like the song, she seemed to be someone I've always, known from a place distant yet so familiar. It was a place I could not identify exactly but one that I felt within me was true," explained Lola Mila to the Manila Mail.

Mila arrived in the United States in 2002 after being accepted as a graduate student in the Drama Therapy Program at Kansas State University. She has a degree in Journalism at the University of the Philippines and is a doctor in expressive arts therapies. She is currently practicing as a therapist at a treatment program for alcoholics and drug users in New Mexico.

She has six children from her past two marriages in the Philippines and seven grandchildren. She was separated from her third husband, an African-American much younger than her when she met Dr. Barcelo who is a lesbian and was single for a long time. Rusty was very cautious about entering into another relationship after a failed romance.

The Filipino American Journey

"I was always aware of my sexuality since I was eight years old and my grandmother who played a key role in my life told me that I needed to be educated because men would never be important to me," Rusty revealed.

Mila describes Rusty as an intelligent, polite, strong, and unique person who is very engaged in the world, who is political and is not afraid to take a stand. Dr. Barcelo is known nationally for her diverse work in education, equality and multi-cultural presentations. She is a Doctor of Philosophy and had served as President of Northern New Mexico College. Currently, she is the Visiting Special Assistant to the Chancellor for Diversity at the University of Illinois at Urbana Champaign.

After their meeting at the Minneapolis Airport, they found themselves emailing and talking on the phone and the deep connection led to visit to Hawaii. "We felt the connection all over again not only physically, but emotionally and spiritually. She asked would you like to be my spouse? I said yes. It was that simple and true," Lola Mila said.

As expected, there were resistance from some friends and other members of her family, but she got the blessings from her only daughter to go ahead while she's still able to enjoy life. "Go Mama, make beautiful memories with her so that when you get older, you can reminisce the many beautiful memories that you have made together," Mila shared.

It was such a liberating experience for two individuals to be together so on July 15, 2015 the couple exchanged commitment vows at the University of the Philippines, Diliman officiated by a babaylan (priestess) and married legally on October 22, 2016 in Minneapolis, Minnesota. For Lola Mila and Dr. Rusty, marriage was something they knew would protect their legal rights, in healthcare and in the right to decide what was best for them. Of course, some people are curious to know who they are as a couple of the same sex. "We get stares, we get questions, we get smiles and friendship, we get admiration, we also get silence and people turning their backs. Rusty and I both decided that we will state our truth, simply and with dignity. We will not hide, we will not be embarrassed, we will not be shy. But we will always be respectful of ourselves and the spaces of others," Lola Mila averred.

Dr. Barcelo believes that there is no boundary when it comes to love. "We are two elders who found each other late in life not because we were lonely but because the spirit of love was so overwhelming that we both let our hearts come together overcoming a myth that old people don't experience all the joys of new and growing love." When we asked Lola Mila how her little grandchildren reacted to her 4th marriage. "My five-year-old granddaughter inquisitively asked "Lola is marrying another Lola! Can I get married to the same woman when I grow up too?"

3

MARYLAND ADVISER SEES HIS ROAD LEADING TO POLITICS

Emmanuel Mejorada Welsh is unfazed by the apparent chaos in American politics. The senior policy adviser to the Maryland Comptroller is convinced his destiny lies in politics, starting from the first time he ran for a seat in the student council in the 7th grade. But for now, he's concentrating on helping Marylanders.

Welsh, 27 of Annapolis, Md. is Senior Policy Adviser for the Maryland Comptroller's Office and the Deputy Chief of Staff. He joined the Comptroller's Office in 2015 as the agency's chief speechwriter and authored hundreds of speeches, legislative testimonies, letters to the editor, and publications for the Comptroller and senior leaders.

"I'm truly humbled by the trust and confidence that the Comptroller placed in me by appointing me as deputy chief of staff of a 1,100-person agency. Each and every day, I have the opportunity to make a difference in the lives of others," he averred.

"The Maryland Comptroller's Office is unique in that not only do we collect over three million tax returns annually, but we also have the responsibility of regulating alcohol, tobacco and motor fuel," he told the Manila Mail.

Before joining the Comptroller's Office, Welsh served as legislative aide to Maryland State Senator James Brochin. He was a graduate research fellow at the William Donald Schaefer Center for Public Policy in Baltimore and received his Master of Public Administration with honors from the University of Baltimore and his Bachelor of Science in Political Science with honors from Towson University.

Welsh was born in Manila but raised in the care of a single mother, Jocelyn Mejorada Welsh who hails from Roxas City, the capital town of Capiz province. They migrated to the United States with his younger brother Jose in 2002 when he was 10 years old and were left under the care of relatives in New Jersey while Mrs. Welsh worked in Maryland.

It was obviously very difficult for Emmanuel to be away from his mom but he also understood that she embodies the values of selflessness, hard work and perseverance. "It was very difficult but my grandmother, uncles and aunts and cousins did so much to help us. Here we were, my brother and me living in a foreign country while our mom was working in Maryland. She would take the train every weekend or every other weekend to see us," he recalled.

Later, Mrs. Welsh met her second husband, the late Patrick T. Welsh who was a Maryland state senator (one of the youngest legislators in Maryland during his time). Mr. Welsh decided to adopt Emmanuel and his brother. "My adoptive father is one of my role models and was very influential in my decision to pursue politics and really made a huge impact in my life. He showed me that public service – despite the unflattering headlines about corruption, greed, and power – can be a noble profession.

"We had a Monday ritual when the legislature was in session. After I did my homework, he would drive me down to Annapolis to watch the State Senate session. He introduced me to his former colleagues and shared stories about what it was like to be someone in his mid-20's who not only defeated incumbents who were backed by powerful political forces in his elections to the House of Delegates and Senate but being a legislator at a young age," he explained.

In addition, Welsh also credits his uncle Manuel Mejorada, an Ilonggo journalist in the Philippines as the person who fanned his interest in politics. "I was always interested and followed politics long before I came to the United States. My uncle Manuel Mejorada, was a leading political and civic leader in Iloilo when I was growing up, and history was always my favorite subject in grade school.

"I can distinctly remember when Joseph Estrada was impeached and can still visualize when he left Malacañang Palace aboard a boat on the Pasig River. It was a dark chapter in the history of the Philippines, and at a young age, I understood the value of having honest, honorable leaders in government office," he declared.

Welsh was only 13 years old when he had his first paying job. His mother and adoptive father worked at a real estate company and he did clerical work like filing and organizing records. Since then he started working from serving ice cream to working as a sales associate at Macy's, Bed, Bath and Beyond, to bussing tables at Red Robin, as an assistant to prominent Baltimore philanthropist, to a number of jobs at Towson's University campus. He worked to pay his bills and continue his dream to finish his education.

The world of politics may be chaotic but for Welsh he sees it as a competitive sport. "It's a battle of who can sway public opinion, but the championship prize is not some trophy or a medal but a political office that allows a person to make a difference in his/her community, state the country and the world.

"I believe both parties have true and sincere intents, and I never question the integrity of leaders and voters who happen to have different viewpoints than mine. I believe in the end that both parties have the same objective of making America a better place, but simply have two differing paths of how to meet that objective," he stressed

"Who knows, you may see my name on a ballot in the near future."

4

SON OF FILIPINO IMMIGRANTS IS DC'S FOREIGN PRESS GATEKEEPER

Foreign journalists working on their credentials or simply mining information at the Foreign Press Center in Washington might have encountered Richard Buangan at one time or another. He is, after all, the Managing Director for International Media overseeing the offices of International Media Engagement, the Foreign Press Centers and the Rapid Response Unit of the US State Department's Bureau of Public Affairs.

The Filipino American Journey

Born and raised in San Diego, CA., Buangan, 42, is the son of Filipino immigrants. His father is Arthur Buangan from Baguio, a former U.S. Navy sailor. His mother Evelyn Buangan is a Certified Public Accountant, an alumna of the University of the East in Manila. Both immigrated in the U.S. during the 1970's and raised their kids in a very diverse community.

"I grew up in several neighborhoods because my father was in the Navy, so we moved around a lot and everywhere I went, I was part of a very diverse community and I never struggled as an Asian American," he revealed to the Manila Mail.

Growing up, he recalled how he always felt content in the library reading and studying while other kids were outside playing sports. He always chose to be inside the house studying, striving for the success of academic accomplishment. Eventually in college he graduated Magna Cum Laude with a baccalaureate in Political Science and Economics from St. Edward's University in Austin, TX.

"My parents instilled in me a hard work ethic to be all you can, to give back to your fellowmen and to take education very seriously because you never know how far it can take you," Buangan explained.

Being a career diplomat wasn't something that Buangan planned. "I wanted to stay in the United States, serve my community here and didn't think much of going overseas or working in another country and speaking a different language. It just became natural. I fell in love with the job probably into my 5th or 6th year of working at the State Department and I took an oath to serve our country whether there's a Democratic or Republican president in the White House."

He started working at the State Department in 1999. Prior to his current assignment, Buangan was Chief of the Public Diplomacy Section of the U.S. Consulate General in Jerusalem managing several programs related to media outreach, education and cultural exchange programs in Jerusalem, the West Bank and Gaza strip. He is fluent in several languages, including French, Spanish and Mandarin Chinese.

Some of his past positions included duties Foggy Bottom as a Staff Officer for Secretaries Colin Powell and Condoleezza Rice. He also became the Vice Consul of the United States Embassy in Paris, France and Third Secretary for Political Affairs/Administrative Affairs in Abidjan.

The Filipino American Journey

Buangan believes that some of the most rewarding aspects of his job are taking young people from different countries and introducing them to the United States. In addition, he works with foreign journalists and helps them report on American politics and society. For him, the media plays a very important role not just in the U.S. but other parts of the world. "We tend to forget that there is more media out there other than New York Times and CNN. There are a lot of media overseas that follow the United States politics, business and culture and my job is to explain all of that to foreign journalists who are from overseas or who maybe here in the United States."

Buangan is very grateful and thankful for the support of his family. As an American, he is proud of his Filipino heritage and can't forget his roots but at the same time loyal to the United States. "As a diplomat and someone who lives overseas, I continue to interact with people from all walks of life," he said.

When asked about his advice for millennials who wants to follow in his footsteps as a foreign service officer, he advised them to "learn that there is life beyond borders that you live. If you travel, don't just travel within your country. Travel overseas and do an exchange program, when you're in high school or college. Learn a different language and learn that there is a different perspective out there. Learn to understand and appreciate different cultures, religions and values system."

5

LOLA'S STORY- A FAMILY'S TALE OF LOVE AND CONFLICT

Alex Tizon, the Pulitzer Prize-winning journalist passed away suddenly of natural causes last March 23 before his final story "My Family's Slave" was published in June by The Atlantic. The story went viral, sparking a debate in the United States and the Philippines. It tells the story of Filipina Eudocia Tomas Pulido known as "Lola" for the Tizon family. She lived with them, virtually a slave for 56 years. The parents of Alex treated Lola terribly even though she cooked, cleaned and raised the kids without pay.

Alex's death left many unanswered questions though he and Lola are not around anymore to defend themselves. It was very difficult for Alex's siblings to speak up. I didn't expect I'd be able to convince Alex's brother,

Rev. Dr. Al Tizon to give a detailed account of Lola's story because he declined numerous requests for interviews. I was therefore privileged to be able to talk to him on my radio show 'Pilipinas sa Amerika' and for the Manila Mail.

Rev. Al Tizon is presently the Executive Minister of Serve Globally based in Chicago, Illinois who oversees the International Ministries of the ECC and travels extensively to lend guidance and support to its 125 personnel around the world including the Philippines, though they don't have personnel (missionaries) but they partner with Jesus Covenant Church in Pasig City and with Acts Integrated Ministries in Quezon City.

He, like his older brother Alex, was born in the Philippines. His family immigrated in the US in 1964 when he was two years old. He is the 3rd of five children of Leticia and Francisco Tizon. "I didn't return until 1989 at age 27. My wife and I, with our then-two children (we ended up having four) went to the Philippines under the auspices of Seattle-based Christian Organization called Action International Ministries," Tizon explained.

"From 1989 to 1998, we lived and worked in the Philippines. I was involved in community development in two squatter communities near the large garbage dump area in Quezon City called Payatas. And then four years later we moved to Zambales province where I continued to engage in community development trying to help people rebuild their lives after the eruption of Mt. Pinatubo, as well as provide pastoral leadership in a young church among the poor in Olongapo City." At age six, Rev. Tizon realized that his parent's treatment of Lola was contrary to Christian values. He remembered feeling bad for Lola, who was getting yelled at for whatever reason and even physical abuse inflicted upon her by his parents. "The volume seemed disproportionate to the fault, if there was any fault at all. The Christian values I began to discover when I came to faith at the age of 17 only reinforced that sense of injustice and indignity that our Lola endured, he recalled."

Growing up Rev. Tizon explained that they never used the term 'slave" to describe Lola's status, but when his brother used it for the story, he and his siblings did not challenge it. To them Lola was more accurately like an indentured servant but "slave" touched a global nerve that has generated important conversations and discussions.

It was at the age of 17 when Rev. Tizon decided to become a Christian minister. It was such a life changing experience, saving him from a life of despair and self -destruction, that he wanted others to experience God's Mercy and love too. "That gratitude translated into a sense of calling from God to share the good news of Christ to others in word and deed," he said.

For Rev. Tizon, the demands of ministry are high and if managed poorly, the ministry could result in emotional burnout, serious marital problems and even divorce, and resentment among children. Some of these demands include having to be available 24/7 for people, resolving conflicts between parishioners, caring for the sick and the dying, maintaining the righteous image of devotion. Thankfully, his wife Janice Tizon has been his source of encouragement and strength. He considers Janice her partner not only in life, but in ministry.

"Her patience, understanding, and sense of common calling in Christ have enabled me to be the best I can be. Together despite our imperfections and despite the high demands of ministry, we raised four children, who are now pretty amazing adults with families of their own," says Rev. Tizon.

Growing up Rev. Tizon shares her fondest memory of "Lola." He has an affectionate collage of memories including her lying beside him as a child rubbing his back when he couldn't sleep; her amazing cooking, her interrogation of their girlfriends and boyfriends, her affirmation after she sat through one of his sermons; her presence in significant events in his life such as his graduations, her fear of caterpillars and her laugh. "I remember when we went to see the movie Jaws together with Lola when it first came out, how she laughed all the way through it. She had no fear of sharks, but caterpillars a different story."

Rev. also recalled some of his memorable moments with Alex including their cross-country bus ride from NYC to Spokane, WA to visit their older brother. Alex was 13 and he was 10 at that time. It includes Alex cheering him on at his high school football games; talking endlessly about girls they met at school and one time they dated the sisters, arguing intensely about politics and religion.

"It includes the year that he and his first wife and daughter spent nine months living with us in Manila. During that time, we wrote several stories together, visited family in the province (including Lola's relatives) and went to church together. He accompanied me a number of times to the squatter community that I served. My memories include going to bookstores with him, drinking good coffee, receiving articles he had written that he's send me. It includes advice he'd give me on my writing projects. I miss him," Rev. Tizon revealed.

Rev. Tizon doesn't believe that any one of them were closer to Lola than the others. He said that Alex was always the master story teller in their family. "No one could have told the story of Lola better than Alex. But again, the story he wrote about Lola was our story. On a scale of 1 to 10, I rate our closeness to Lola an 11! She was our everything – our mother, our father, our confidante, our disciplinarian, our friend. One result to Alex's story for the siblings was that we ended up have to relieve the grief of losing her in 2011. It was double grief for us: losing our brother and "re-losing" our Lola."

To live knowing that his parents enslaved a person like Lola haunts Rev. Tizon and his four other siblings who struggled of guilt for decades. Lola was treated poorly and was not free. "It haunts us to be honest. We all have demons, we struggle (metaphorically speaking) to this day as a result of having lived the daily contradiction or tension of the situation. We loved our parents. We loved our Lola." he said sadly.

Many times, the Tizon siblings tried to intervene and talk to their parents about their treatment of Lola and they could all wish they could have done more. "My brother's article described the first time he confronted Mom about Lola, and how it ended in a huge argument. Well, each of us has story or two like that. In addition to arguing with our parents, we also urged Lola to leave; we said that we'd help her go back to the Philippines but she refused, saying that Mom needed her and that she promised Mom's father (our grandfather) that she stayed with her." He added that his Mom and Lola had a strange relationship, a co-dependent one as his psychologist friends would say. His Mom had the upper hand, but their relationship formed in such a way that they needed each other. "Mom needed Lola to take care of her and Lola needed Mom to fulfill a tragic sense of purpose. I do believe that they loved each other in awful, distorted kind of way."

For the Tizons, the backlash to their family after the story was published is part of the media sensationalism that is worth discussing. "I did not appreciate the negative backlash that also came with the media attention, but that sort of thing is part of the package of anything worth discussing. However, I admitted that the backlash this time happens to be quite personal. It hurts me but I understand it," says Rev. Tizon.

From his point of view, he believes critics have reacted to the surface of the story and didn't bother to dig deeper, take seriously the complexities of any human story, understand the nuances of word usage (e.g., slave) etc. "Like all of us, who are prone to judge others, they seem to have forgotten the teaching of Jesus who said, "Why do you see the speck in your neighbor's eye, but do not notice the log that is in your own eye?" (Matthew 7:3) before his death, Alex has been talking about this story as the one he was meant to write. "That says a lot for someone who wrote many stories," Tizon said.

"We are glad he wrote it. He wrote what we all felt. He wrote our story. And then he died. When The Atlantic asked us if we still wanted to publish it, it felt dishonorable to our brother's memory to say No. Without hesitation, we said 'Yes,' because it was a story worth telling and it honored the memory of Tomas Alex Tizon," the author of his family's secret life and the life of their beloved servant, Lola.

6

THE SAGA OF ALEX AND LOLA

"There is an interest in making the story into a movie," disclosed Melissa Tizon, the widow of the late Pulitzer-Prize winning journalist Alex Tizon, author of the essay "My Family's Slave".

The article for The Atlantic told the story of Eudocia Tomas Pulido known as Lola who lived with Alex's family for 56 years as a virtual slave. "Alex struggled with Lola's story for 5-6 years because it was very difficult story to write, very painful and required a lot of soul searching for him to understand the complexity of the relationship," she averred.

And now people in Hollywood and the Philippines have been talking to her about putting his story on the screen but there's been no final decision yet," she told the Manila Mail in an exclusive interview.

It's been seven months since Alex passed, and Melissa still grieves the loss every day. She misses her husband a lot and thinks about him all the time. They have two kids Dylan, 26, from Alex's earlier marriage and Maya, 17, their biological daughter now in high school.

Recently, the Tizons spread some of Alex's ashes in one of his favorite beaches in Seattle, Wa. Alex died of natural causes on March 23, 2017. "We were in Seattle and he was in Eugene, Oregon on the day that he died. What happened is that the girls and I would call and text him every day and we realized that we couldn't get a hold of him, then he wasn't responding so I finally called the police in Oregon to check on him and they found him in bed and he had died peacefully in his sleep," Melissa shared with the Manila Mail. Alex died from what Filipinos call "bangungot."

Melissa described her husband as an amazing person who was so encouraging and had a lot of charm and charisma. "He loves talking to his readers about the stories that he wrote and loves to connect with people. He believes that every person has an important story to tell and even if it's just meeting someone in a conversation or at the party or at the coffee shop. I wish, he was alive to do this interview with you. People really liked him. He used his God-given talent to the best of his ability, he never compromised and he puts all his energy to being a writer, it's a risk to be a writer but he managed to do what he wanted in life.

"He was a great dad, husband and friend. I have been very lucky to be married to him for 19 years. I'm just really proud of him for being the kind of person who really cared about other people, who really tried to get to know people. I personally tend to be a little superficial like I mind my own business but Alex really wanted to know people and I think that's the quality about him that I really admired."

Melissa recalled that when she was dating Alex he had told her about Lola, that she was a grandmother or a great aunt who raised him and his brothers and sisters but she didn't know the extent of abuses that Lola suffered from Alex's parents and grandfather. "I didn't know all the details of the abuses until I read the draft of the story. She was such an important person in his life. I heard so much about her before I actually met her. Lola was in her late 60's when they met. Her first meeting with Lola was warm and wonderful. She endured a lot in her life and yet she never let that stop her from being happy and she never let that stop her from caring other people."

She also remembered one weekend when she went to Alex's mother house where she was supposed to sleep in Lola's bedroom. She found it so weird, surprising and strange that a grandmother was supposed to be respected but was kicked out of her bedroom. She ended losing an argument with Alex's mother.

The Filipino American Journey

Melissa believes that her husband will always be remembered for the story that he wrote in the Atlantic. It was a story that he told her, he was born to write and this was his epic story. He loved Lola like his mother and he really wanted to tell her story and this is what he wanted to accomplish in life and he did it. Unfortunately, Alex passed away before his essay was published.

When Alex's mother died, the Tizon siblings talked to Lola about what she wanted to do next, if she wanted to move back in the Philippines to be with her family or maybe build a house. She chose to be with her and Alex.

"We have a home just a north of Seattle, Washington. She came and moved in with us. When she came with us, we were very clear in not having her as a worker. We don't want her to work anymore, we just wanted her to relax and enjoy the final years of her life and she did," Melissa explained.

Alex's family didn't anticipate the backlash to the story though 90 percent has been very positive. "I didn't have any idea that it would be this big and the 2nd most read article in the history of the Atlantic magazine which has been around 150 years. Alex used the word slave in the story because he didn't want to whitewash anything, he wanted his story to be accurate," Melissa said.

The misery of Lola made him famous and, perhaps denied him in death, the solace of seeing the impact of his work.

7

LOVE TRANSCENDS TIME, DISTANCE, HISTORY FOR COUPLE

Love, barbs attest, transcends time and distance. And it was for **Leocita and Ray Sauter** who met in Iloilo in 1985, and kept their torch burning across the seas, the tumultuous turns of Philippine history and life's own twists until fate finally intervened and they would come face to face again, in Texas almost three decades later.

It was in February 1985 when 20-year-old Leocita Talanas met 20-year-old, Ray Sauter at the Iloilo City Hall. She had a bubbly personality, bordering on the boisterous. Ray was a US Navy sailor assigned in Guam but visiting the Philippines for the first time to accompany a friend who was getting married to his Ilongga girlfriend. Leocita was a working student and casual employee of the city government. She was in charge of processing marriage licenses at the Mayor's office.

"She was quite talkative and eager to share with me many of her interests and passions. I learned she was active in KB or Kabataang Barangay (a community youth organization) and that she was a First Lieutenant in the Philippine Army Reserve. Seeing that I was a mere enlisted man in the U.S. Navy recently promoted to Petty Officer second Class), I was quite impressed and just a bit intimidated to be interacting with someone who was a commissioned officer," Ray recalled.

For Leocita, Ray epitomized the "ideal man"- handsome, intelligent and very well-mannered. They developed their relationship as "pen pals." He would write to her almost every day and call whenever his ship would dock.

In 1986, they met again in Subic Bay. Ray was deployed with the USS Enterprise Battle Group which at the time called on Subic Bay. He made a contact with Leocita to meet him at the port. "It was during this time I first felt the sparks fly and I realized what a special and wonderful lady she was. I confessed my love and sincerity and conviction I had not felt for any other or anyone since. It was that Saturday night that we had the photo taken of the two of us - the only one remaining. It was the night I realized I wanted to spend the rest of my life with this lady, it was also the night before (Pres. Ferdinand) Marcos would be ousted by the People Power Revolution," Ray explained.

Ray and Leocita talked about the possibility of marriage but he had not formally popped the question. After their wonderful evening together, he dropped her off and went back to the base. He woke up the next morning and got ready for church. He had a new custom-tailored barong, making him one of the best dressed men in Olongapo City, looking forward to what he thought would be the best day of his life. He knew he was in love with Leocita, fairly sure that he was going to ask her to marry him that day.

"I was just about to walk out when the division officer of our detachment knocks on our door and tells us that we need to pack up and get back to the ship. A military coup was anticipated and martial law' has been declared. Everything was locked down and no one was getting off the base," he remembered.

"All I could think about was that Leocita was stranded out in town with no means to get back home. I didn't get to talk with her directly and as the situation was classified at that time, I had no idea whether she made it safely back to Iloilo," Ray said.

He wrote letters to Leocita trying to reach out to her but all the letters just stacked up and their communication was cut off for 27 years.

Leocita tried to move on with her life and got pregnant with five kids. She married a man who came from one of the prominent families in Iloilo; however, she was treated unfairly by her in-laws and was unhappy.

Each time she got pregnant her in-laws would her send her husband to other places so she ended up raising the kids alone.

On July 9, 2001, Leocita arrived in the U.S. to attend a seminar as part of the Iloilo City delegation. She decided to stay in America and work as a caregiver. In January 2004, she met a Filipino-American disc jockey Rod Elston. He married Leocita and gave her a green card. Elston died of cancer in January 2013. Leocita was able to petition her kids and was already earning well as a caregiver when she got addicted to gambling and other vices while living in Los Angeles, CA. Ray on the other hand, was married for 20 years and has a daughter. That union ended with divorce in 2013.

"I was going through the final phases of my divorce and just moved out of my house into an apartment and decided to make everything official by changing my Facebook relationship status from "married" to "separated." The very next day, I got a friend request from Leocita. We communicated a little via text messaging," he disclosed.

It happened Leocita was in Texas at that time to take care of an ailing friend. She befriended Ray on Facebook out of curiosity, just to find out how he was doing after more than two decades of not hearing from one another. "I went to Galleria (in Houston) without any expectations other than to meet and visit an old friend. I certainly thought the feelings had changed. I was expecting merely us to be friends," he said.

"While we were sitting at the food court, she took out the photos I had given her years ago and said she always kept them. I couldn't help but think what a wonderful life I would've had with her," Ray mused.

As sparks flew once more, Ray and Leocita decided to do what they could have imagined that February morning, 28 years earlier. In March 15, 2014 they took their vows as husband and wife. "Those sparks still have not subsided," Ray declared.

8

FAMILY ADOPTS TETRAPLEGIC GIRL FROM PHILIPPINES, FACES CHALLENGES WITH LOVE, FAITH

It took a lot of courage, faith and hope for couple Jason and Adrianne Stewart of Utah, to adopt a little girl from the Philippines named Maria who was born without limbs and arms and has the rare congenital disorder called Tetra-Amelia Syndrome.

Maria was placed in Chosen Children Village, an orphanage for children with special needs in Silang, Cavite when she was only six months old.

There was not enough information about the medical background of the girl except that she was born without limbs, legs and arms. The Stewart adoption story went viral on YouTube after Adrianne and Jason documented and told the story of how they adopted their youngest child. The video was reposted in the Facebook Page of a popular site "Love What Matters" that shares inspiring stories and has been viewed close to a million viewers. Internet and other media outlets like CNN, CBS, Fox News and other international news organizations interviewed the family. Their story has been shared almost all over the world. The Stewarts said that they shared their story to inspire others to adopt children with special needs. I was lucky enough to be one of the journalists whom they granted an interview for my radio show "Pilipinas sa Amerika" and for "Manila Mail."

Personally, I feel like I bonded with the family as I interviewed Jason and Adrianne Stewart. Maria was blowing kisses on the phone while I was talking to her parents and she was learning to talk in English. She bonded so well with her elder sisters and older brother. Adrianne says, her other kids don't even think Maria has a physical disability. To them, she is just a normal and adorable little sister who likes to giggle and play with stuffed animals and would spend most of her time coloring pictures using a mouthpiece that was especially made for her.

Maria was placed in Chosen Children Village, an orphanage for children with special needs in Silang, Cavite when she was only six months old.

She also loves music and has a loud voice. The parents think their youngest daughter might be a singer one day. "We have two biological daughters, 13 and 11 years old and after we adopted our son Joshua Stewart five years ago, we decided our family wasn't complete so we decided to adopt again in the Philippines. It was difficult and tough at first, thinking we are going to adopt a kid without arms and legs. I don't even know if we could do it," says Adrianne.

They were anxious but excited to welcome the little girl in their family. It was the picture of Maria smiling that captured the hearts of Adrianne and Jason. "She has the most beautiful smile and so adorable and we fell in love with her. We just knew that we needed to make her part of our family," the couple said. Adrianne Stewart used to work as an Occupational Therapist before she decided to become a full-time housewife. Jason works as an installer for a cable company in Utah. He speaks Tagalog. He learned the language when he lived in the Philippines for two years as a missionary for Church of Christ of the Latter-Day Saints and fell in love with the Filipino people and the culture. "Filipinos are great. I was just a stranger in the Philippines but they are always happy, kind and willing to give," Jason explained.

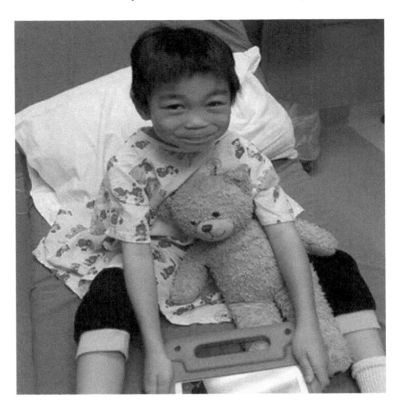

Maria amazes her adopted parents of what she has learned to do all on her own. She greatly impressed everyone when she learned how to manipulate and control her wheelchair by going up and down the halls without any help from her parents. She now goes to preschool a couple of days per week. In addition, she receives occupational and speech therapy.

The family is also processing the adoption papers of another 9-year-old girl with special needs from the Philippines whom they are planning to adopt next year. But they now face more adversity; they learned only recently that Joshua has cancer.

They adopted Joshua in the Philippines in 2012 when he was a year old. It has taken them a while to process the whole thing and what has also changed their life. "Joshua had fallen ill in late March and we thought it was a flu. After a few days we took him to the doctor and found out that he had a strep throat, after several days of medicine for that, he was still not feeling well and did not appear recovering. Then he was first diagnosed with anemia and admitted to the hospital."

"On April 4, the doctor met with us about some tests that they were running on him because things did not meet the normal results. This is where the big news hit us hard. Our son was diagnosed with AML or Acute Myeloid Leukemia. By the end of the week, he had begun his chemotherapy treatment." The family doesn't know what the future holds. While they are aware of the possibilities, they choose to focus on the positive. The family regularly keeps in touch with this writer and been giving updates about Joshua.

"Joshua is a fighter and we have a lot of faith and hope that he will get through this. He is doing good. He is back home and regaining his strength before going back for Round 2 of chemotherapy. It has been a really nice break having him home and letting him run around and be a kid again. Joshua is scheduled to get his bone marrow tested to see if the 1st round of chemo got rid of all the cancer. If they find no cancer left then he will just continue three more rounds of chemotherapy to keep him in remission and if they find there is cancer still, then he will need a bone marrow transplant," Adrianne shared in her last message.

Life for them goes on with challenges, greater than most families face, but that will not break their bonds of love. Tested in so many ways, their faith uplifts their spirits and their friends have offered to help with them with their finances by starting a GoFundMe page for the Stewarts.

Love, faith and family can overcome a lot.

9

THE TRINIDAD FAMILY'S ILL-FATED JOURNEY HOME

Editor's Note: On July 6, 61-year-old Audie Trinidad of Teaneck, New Jersey, and his daughters — Kaitlyn, 20, Danna, 17, and 13-year-old twins Allison and Melissa —were killed on a Delaware highway in their 1999 Toyota Sienna minivan when a Ford pickup truck going the opposite direction crossed over the median and slammed into their vehicle. Mary Rose Trinidad, 53, wife and mother, was the lone survivor of the tragic accident. She underwent four surgeries for multiple injuries, considered "non-threatening," and remains in stable condition in a hospital. She is waiting to be transferred to a hospital closer to the family's home. Meanwhile, funeral services are put on hold.

They were a close family of six, happily spending their vacation on a beach in Ocean City, four hours away from where they live, in Teaneck, New Jersey. They were on their way home: dad, on the driver's seat, mom right beside him and their four daughters in the minivan's back seats. After stopping for lunch, their last meal together, they resumed their journey home.

And then it happened swiftly, prompting Delaware State Police Master Corporal Melissa Jaffee, who was at the scene of the accident, to share her horror with the media: "To lose four children in a crash … it's just unheard of."

An American Story
Audie Trinidad, who was named after Audie Murphy (a decorated World War II infantryman who earned 28 medals for combat heroism) came

to the United States in 1987. He served in the U.S. Navy for seven years aboard the USS Mount Whitney, a communications ship named for the tallest mountain peak in California. He was so proud of the ship that he sent a poster of it to his family in the Philippines. After his navy stint, he went on to work for the U.S. Postal Service. He settled in Teaneck, where he and his wife raised a family of four girls.

"He was proud to be an American," said his brother, Daniel, who lives in Miami. "That's why he joined the Navy. Audie's biggest dream was to see all her daughters finish college, so they can have a better life; and to grow old gracefully with his wife.

"My brother tells me all the time how blessed and lucky he is to have a wonderful, loving wife, a good mother; and having respectful children and that he couldn't ask for more. My brother is also a pleasant man. If you need something you wouldn't have to ask twice. He was very helpful, cheerful, good-natured, God-fearing man, close to being a perfect father."

Daniel wished he was able to speak to his brother before the tragic accident. "Father's Day was the last time we spoke but we kept in touch almost on a daily basis via text," he says. "He was the best brother, friend and husband anyone could ask for."

'All gone in the blink of an eye.'

In an interview with the New York Post shortly after the tragedy, Daniel said: "How are you going to bury five people at the same time? This is like a tragedy a hundred times over. They're a God-fearing family. They go to church. Now, they're all gone in the blink of an eye."

Except for Mary Rose, who grew up in Mindoro province. She is still nursing her wounds but is expected to make it. She is a nurse at Beth Israel Hospital in New York City, where she met her husband. The couple have been married since 1995.

Kaitlyn, who went by Nikki, was a nursing student at the College of Mount Saint Vincent in the Bronx. She had just graduated from college. Her 17-year-old sister, Danna, a member of the high school volleyball team, was going to be a senior at Teaneck High School. The twins, Melissa and Allison, would have entered eighth grade at Thomas Jefferson Middle School in Teaneck.

His entire family felt the loss, including the girls' grandmother. She lived with the Trinidad family, Daniel said. She just lost all her grandchildren living in the United States. The grandmother is having a hard time with the five sudden losses, he said. For Daniel, he remembers the last conversation he had with his brother.

A community comes together: News of the devastating tragedy drew an outpouring of prayers, messages, acts of kindness, fundraisers and other forms of public support from the tightly-knit Teaneck community and across the nation.

"Everyone that I knew who went to high school and middle school with them, I can see that they were a part of the Teaneck family. They touched our lives in many ways," the mayor said. A family friend, Linda Douglas, immediately set up a GoFundMe for the family. She said her daughter and Danna Trinidad were best friends in high school. They were about to start their senior year together in New Jersey.

Douglas added that Danna's father was "always the dad to pick everyone up in the minivan … We traded off, but no matter whose sweet 16 it was, you could always count on Audie."

As of July 14, the GoFundMe page has exceeded its original goal of $250,000 in one week. It has now grown to $267, 744 as more social media users have donated for the medical and funeral expenses. Anyone wishing to donate can click on the Go-Fund-Me link.

On Sunday, the loss of the Trinidad family was keenly felt at St. Anastasia's Roman Catholic Church, where the family members were longtime parishioners and Audie Trinidad had served as an usher. Candles and flowers were set up along the pew that would normally be occupied by the family at the 11:30 a.m. Mass. Many parishioners were moved to tears as they remembered the father and daughters.

For its part, the Philippine Consulate in New York City is working with the Department of Foreign Affairs to facilitate travel arrangements of relatives from the Philippines, notably Mary Rose's brother, Paul Ballocanag. The consulate has also offered to provide legal assistance, as needed. "We have alerted our contacts in the legal community, and if called upon, we can suggest the names of reputable lawyers who may be able to assist," said Philippine Consul Kerwin Orville C. Tate. "We are doing what we can to help the family during this moment of grief. It gives us comfort, knowing we are not alone," Daniel said.

Daniel adds that the family is looking for the best lawyer as they are planning to file charges against Maryland resident Alvin S. Hubbard Jr., 44, driver of the pickup truck that slammed into Trinidad's minivan. "We want Hubbard to be held responsible for the deaths of my brother and four nieces," Daniel told Manila Mail. News reports that the four sisters were not wearing seat belts prompted reminders in social media to strap on your seat belts and save lives.

With a family of four girls, two young children and two about to bloom into successful adults, and a proud father, their deaths no doubt remind us all that every family, no matter how tightly tied and happy, is still fragile and mortal. For Mary Rose Trinidad we can only wonder in sympathy how one recovers from a sudden loss that severe.

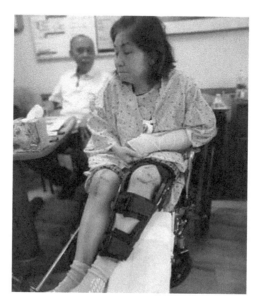

10

LONE SURVIVOR OF DELAWARE CAR ACCIDENT SEEKS JUSTICE FOR FAMILY MEMBERS

Editor's Note: On July 6, 61-year-old Audie Trinidad of Teaneck, New Jersey, and his daughters — Kaitlyn, 20, Danna, 17, and 13-year-old twins Allison and Melissa —were killed on a Delaware highway in their 1999 Toyota Sienna minivan when a Ford pickup truck going the opposite direction crossed over the median and slammed into their vehicle. They were on their way home after a week's vacation in Ocean City, Maryland. Mary Rose Trinidad, 53, wife and mother, was the lone survivor of the tragic accident. She underwent four surgeries for multiple injuries. After being hospitalized for almost six weeks, she is now recovering at the Kessler Rehabilitation Center in New Jersey. Funeral services for Mary Rose's husband and four children were held on August 11. Manila Mail staff writer Josie Moralidad Ziman had an exclusive phone interview with Mrs. Trinidad on August 12.

The Filipino American Journey

As a reporter, my interview with Mary Rose Ballocanag Trinidad is one of the most heartbreaking and difficult interviews I've ever done in my journalism career. It is because the tragedy that happened to her and her family is very traumatic. I had to be sensitive and gentle with my questions.

Mary Rose said she couldn't remember much about the accident. "I woke up in pain, pinned in my seat and saw a lot of people trying to get me out of the car," she recalls vaguely. "When I turned to look at my husband, he was slumped on the driver's seat and I couldn't see his face. I kept asking where my kids are. They just told me they were working on them. Then I passed out." In and out of consciousness, she only remembers being transported by a helicopter to the hospital. She is able to recollect memories of their family vacation in Ocean City and the trip home. Her four daughters were all lying down and sleeping inside their mini-van, without their seatbelts on.

Mary Rose describes her family as very close knit: "We go to church together as a family. We travel together, and we do everything together. My husband Audie goes to church more and the kids go with him when I'm at work. He would jump at everything and bring whatever the kids need in school."

She says she met him in New York City, introduced to each other by a mutual friend. "He is very loving; he spoiled me and the kids. Whatever we ask from him, he would give everything to us. He is God-fearing. Family is his top priority."

For Mary Rose, her four daughters are the most loving and sweetest girls. "Every day they say, 'I love you' and 'thank you' for doing and buying this or that. Not a day goes by without them saying 'I love you' to me, especially the twins. They hugged and kissed me before I go to work." Mary Rose is a night shift nurse at Beth Israel Medical Center in Manhattan.

When asked about her fondest memory with her family, she points out the love and affection everyone had for each other. "Kaitlyn is very sweet and loving. She always called to tell what she needs in school, and checked everyone. Danna is very friendly. She has a lot of friends. She's the high maintenance among the four. She loves shoes. If I don't give it to her, Dad will give it to her when she gets straight A's in school. The twins, Allyson and Melissa, when they're not doing anything, they like to dance with their cousins."

Last Saturday, mourners from all walks of life – notably from the Filipino community – joined Mary Rose in paying their final respect and farewell to her husband and four daughters. The funeral service was held in the Rothman Center Arena at Fairleigh Dickinson University, Hackensack, New Jersey where the five caskets were draped in white cloths. A portrait of each family member was placed on the coffin with flowers.

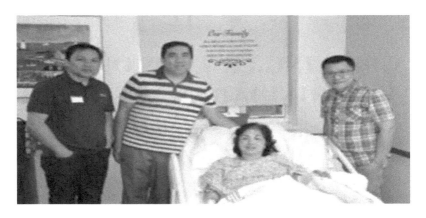

After the funeral mass, attended by almost a thousand mourners, a folded US military flag was given to Mary Rose in honor of her late husband, Audie. He served in the U.S. Navy aboard the USS Mount Whitney. After his navy stint, he went on to work for the U.S. Postal Service. He settled in Teaneck, New Jersey, where he and his wife raised a family of four girls.

Mary Rose explains that she decided to hold the funeral to put her family to rest. "It's been more than six weeks, it's time for them to rest. I can move better than before and I can sit on the wheelchair. I'm grateful to my family and to all the people who are helping me go through this painful time in my life. They have not abandoned me."

The grieving mom who is still recovering from multiple injuries is going through an extensive physical therapy every day. When asked where she gets the strength to move on with her life now, she says "My church, and lots of family and friends who are always behind me. The least I can do is to be strong for everyone. I know my family wants me to be strong also."

Since the horrific accident happened more than four weeks ago, no charges have been filed against the driver, Alvin S. Hubbard Jr., 40, of East New Market, Maryland. Last month during the press conference at the Kessler Rehabilitation Center, Mary Rose declared that she is seeking justice for the death of her family. "I'm dying inside over and over again. Justice will not bring them back, but we will be in a safer place," she said.

A Facebook community page "Justice for Mary Rose Ballocanag Trinidad" has been created in support of Mary Rose and justice for her family. "It's frustrating," Mary Rose says of the police investigation. "I feel like nothing was done. It's been six weeks already and still no updates. To the driver of the truck who killed five people, he should be held responsible for what he did. I want justice for my family."

Mary Rose is thinking of establishing a scholarship foundation to honor her family, to keep alive the memory of their goodness as best she can.

11

GRIEVING FRIENDS OF KAITLYN TRINIDAD SHARE THEIR MEMORIES

Editor's Note: On July 6, 20-year-old Kaitlyn Trinidad, her sisters — Danna, 17, and 13-year-old twins Allison and Melissa, and their father, 61-year-old Audie Trinidad —were killed on a Delaware highway in their 1999 Toyota Sienna minivan when a Ford pickup truck going the opposite direction crossed over the median and slammed into their vehicle. Their mother, Mary Rose Trinidad, 53, was the lone survivor. The family was on their way home to Teaneck, NJ, after a week's vacation in Ocean City, when the tragic accident happened. Kaitlyn was a senior nursing student at the College of Mount Saint Vincent in the Bronx. Kaitlyn's friends share their fond recollections and memories.

I found out about the accident from a family friend who messaged me on Instagram," Steven, a Filipino-Cambodian, recalls. "I was just shocked and sick to the stomach. I lost it. She was my first true love, my soul mate. I didn't fully realize how I felt about her until she was gone. I love her to death. And I would trade places with her if I could."

Steven met Kaitlyn in a lounge on their college campus. They were introduced to each other by mutual friends. "We have been together since October 26, 2016, but we decided to keep our relationship a secret because of how strict both our parents are," Steven says. "They want us to stay focused on our academics. They would have been worried if they found out we were dating."

Steven explains that as students he and Kaitlyn are passionate about finishing their college education and be the best of whatever they want to be in the future. "We were determined to pursue our nursing careers," he says. "We never gave in or gave up when times were rough. She pushed me to excel. She never settled for average or passing grades. She made me aim for A's. She hated it when she would get a B in class and I started to feel the same."

Kaitlyn's last message for Steven was full of love and assurances that she deeply loves him and that she will facetime him when she gets home from Ocean City. He remembers that Kaitlyn was very happy when he got her a promise ring in December last year, which she never took off. "I wish I told her then that I loved her," Steven says. "And not just saying it but telling her why. Just to thank her for all she has done for me. She was my home away from home. I just wanted to tell her that I'm sorry for all the times we argued because of my insecurity and that I'm sorry for telling her not to get me gifts because I feel like I didn't deserve it. I just wish I told her then what she meant to me, that I wanted to marry her one day."

'An amazing ate'

Filipino American Frances Verdeflor, 20, is Kaitlyn's roommate and closest friend. She describes Kaitlyn as very compassionate, caring responsible, hardworking and a dedicated student. "She had a little bit of OCD compared to her sister Danna," Frances says. "Kaitlyn was more focused on her school life more than anything else. I admired her extreme work-ethic and determination. She would always be at least two weeks ahead when it came to reading her assignments. When she received a low grade on a nursing exam she would freak out and start calculating the grades she needed on the next three exams. She and Steven would study together, or study in different locations at the same time. She would always find time to help other people especially struggling freshman nursing students."

Frances said her mind was going in circles after she learned of Kaitlyn's death. It was very difficult for her to accept that Kaitlyn's gone. "A few of my friends had attempted to contact me through text, phone calls and facetime, but I was asleep," she recalls. "My friend Maria was able to reach me at 2:00 A.M. through facetime. I was concerned because it looked like she had been crying and after reading the text messages I received I was so confused. She told me:

'Fran, Kat got into a really bad car accident and she didn't make it. I'm so sorry Fran.' And I asked her if this was a prank or a joke and she told me 'No, I'm sorry Fran, her sisters and dad passed away too.' And that's when I broke down and cried. I just couldn't believe it."

Recently, Frances visited Kaitlyn's mother at the hospital and she told her some of their family stories: "She told me how Danna loved shoes and how she probably got that trait from her Dad, Tito Audie. He would have the same shoes but in two different colors. The twins I know would steal Kaitlyn's clothes or ask Kaitlyn for her clothes. They all looked up to Kaitlyn and she was an amazing Ate."

Frances also revealed that Kaitlyn was always proud of her loving and hardworking parents and that she was afraid to disappoint them. "She worshipped her parents and adored her little sisters," Frances says. "She would tell me how her mom worked so hard during overnight shifts at the hospital while her father struggled to make the twins Allison and Melissa and Danna finish their work and go to bed early. I knew she valued her family and education."

"She had such a big heart.'

Filipino-American Maria Hofbauer is another close friend of Kaitlyn. She explained that Kaitlyn is a friend you can always count on –

patient, mature and someone who always had a reasonable explanation and rationale. "I remember going to school and I had no friends initially. I felt left out. Kaitlyn, on the other hand, had lots of friends. She was the first to approach me and invite me to share a Filipino dish that she cooked. I really appreciate her for that and we became close ever since."

Maria adds that Kaitlyn always valued her relationship with Steven. "She loved Steven so much, she was always there for him and they were a power couple. They were each other's best friends," she says.

Maria believes that though Kaitlyn's life was cut short, she made the most out of her short life. "Kaitlyn definitely seemed quiet and timid from the outside but once you got to know her, she was so much fun and loving," Maria recalls. "She had such a big heart. She also had so much respect for her parents, she wanted to make them proud. They would always come visit her and bring her favorite *lasagna*. She impacted my life in a way I didn't realize. I'm going to miss her so much."

Kaitlyn Trinidad's tragic death left many of her friends feeling a sense of pain and loss. It hurts them to know that the life of a young woman – so full of love, laughter and promise – had been cut senselessly short.

Kaitlyn Trinidad (RIP)
5/12/98 - 7/06/18

12

JO KOY'S INVISIBLE STAGE PARTNER

Whenever you watch a performance by stand-up comic and social media star Joseph Glenn Herbert – better known as Jo Koy – you might wonder if there weren't two of them on the stage – the comedian and his mother Josie Harrison, a Quezon City native who obviously casts a huge influence on his 46-year-old son.

Mrs. Josie Harrison, 70, has always been the center of Jo Koy's acts whenever the Filipino-American comedian is performing in the Unites States and other countries. Talking with the Manila Mail, she described her youngest son as a very kind, generous, loving funny, humble and respectful person.

"We are so much alike in personality, we face our daily life with a smile, we look at any given situation with a positive outlook," she explained.

Jo Koy was only 13 years old when his parents divorced. He is the third child in the family. The eldest is Robert Herbert, Rowena Hazel Cook, Joseph and Gemma Herbert Simmons his adopted sister from the Philippines.

His biological father is Jack Herbert who is retired from the U.S. Air Force. She met him when she was working in Vietnam as an office manager for a Filipino band. Mrs. Harrison is candid about her family life raising four kids as a single parent. "I faced my life with strength and determination that my children will be raised with Filipino traditions and culture while respecting American culture," she averred.

"I went to school on my own. I started from the bottom up. I worked 2 jobs to provide for the need of my 4 children. A banker during the day for Wells Fargo and a cashier/hostess at Denny restaurant at night. I did everything on my own," she added.

Mrs. Harrison explained that she prodded Jo Koy at a young age because she wanted him to lead a different kind of life. She got pregnant at an early age and wasn't able to finish college. "I emphasized to him to focus on professions such as being a nurse, doctor or lawyer. I made it clear to him that with these professions, he could be assured of a comfortable and secured life."

However, Jo Koy decided to take a different path and dropped out in college and did some odd jobs from working as a store clerk to being a stand-up comedian in Las Vegas. He was discovered by a talent coordinator from Los Angeles which landed him his first television appearance at the Black Entertainment Television or BET. The nickname Jo Koy was given to him when he was growing up by his Aunt Evelyn, Mrs. Harrison's sister.

Whenever Jo Koy is on the stage he pokes fun at his Filipino heritage, culture and values. The subject of his jokes has always been about family particularly his mother Josie. When asked if she gets upset, she responds "I actually feel proud, great and excited. I don't mind because it's a real story.

"I am very proud of my son. He is now one of the top comedians in America and a millionaire. During his early comedy adventure, I wrote jokes on yellow stickers and stuck it on his bedroom door. Also, he performed in a small lounge here in Las Vegas somewhere around the University of Nevada Las Vegas or UNLV campus. It's at the Bugzy, he didn't get a good reaction when he delivered his first punchline," Mrs. Harrison recalled.

One of Mrs. Harrison's unforgettable experiences occurred when Jo Koy was starting his career as a comedian. "He was at home during the early days of his comedy career, one night I was watching TV when all of a sudden Jo Koy came rushing to our family room wearing nothing but his Fruit of the Loom underwear. He was pretending to be playing a guitar and he was singing the song that
Tom Cruise sang in the movie "Risky Business" and I just laughed so hard," she said.

She believes that there is celebrity blood in their family. She was a former radio host in Las Vegas. Her own biological mother Justina Gonzales was once a movie actress in the Philippines; her other daughter is a singer in Las Vegas. "My mother is "bolera" (joker) and Jo Koy likes to imitate the actors on the TV and he loves comedy shows. We like to joke each other in the family."

She's overwhelmed by the popularity of his son with so many sold out shows "I can't imagine the status of my son right now. I am in a dream right now. He bought a million-dollar house and I can't believe it, my son is a millionaire right now doing comedy," she said.

For Mrs. Harrison, this is now her proudest moment as a mother. She and her second husband, a retired army soldier and postal service worker are enjoying all the generosity and love of their children. "We can sit back and not worry about their existence because they are all financially well. I think I've done a good job raising my kids," she said.

When I asked her what's the funniest thing Jo Koy said to her as a mother? "That he still hasn't met anyone who's been in America for so long and still can't say his name right," she says of the son she still calls "Josep".

13

PINOY NURSE TURNS HOBBY TO FASHION ROMP

Michael Seneriches is a 43-year-old Ilonggo nurse who works on daily wages at two medical facilities in San Francisco, Ca. But that's not what landed him in the news – fashion is a hobby and that landed him a gig at one of the world's most prestigious fashion shows – New York Fashion Week last Sept. 10 at Piers 59, Chelsea Piers in New York City.

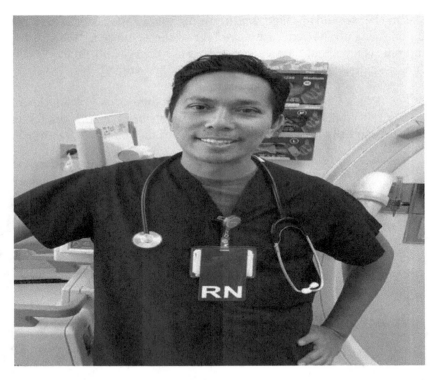

Seneriches, originally from Mandurriao in Iloilo City, Philippines first came to the United States as a tourist in 1996 and eventually decided to emigrate in Chicago where he pursued a career in nursing. He currently works on per diem basis as a clinic nurse at Kaiser Permanente and as a pre-admission testing nurse at Sutterhealth CPMC.

He is a self-taught fashion designer who took some basic sewing classes. "Filmmaking was my first passion and the move to California was sort of part of the goal to be near Hollywood. However, I also started taking interest in Photography (specifically Fashion Designing), and the spark grew into a passion. I started taking basic lessons here and there and started making dresses for fun with some friends," he told the Manila Mail.

He joined the SFFAMA (San Francisco Fashion and Merchant Alliance) in 2010 as a volunteer. One day during the orientation, the organizer announced that he needed more designers for an upcoming show. Without hesitation, Seneriches approached the organizer and showed samples of his work. He presented his first collection as an amateur designer in San Francisco and has since continued to participate in SFFAMA's shows every year until 2012 when he auditioned for the Bravo's produced reality TV show "Project Runway." He got through the initial stages of the selection process, and almost made it to the final 16 that was going to New York.

"Unfortunately, I didn't make it to the Final 16, and that was really a big blow to my dreams of being in New York Fashion Week. I continued to design dresses and join shows in San Francisco, until in December 2016 when I got an email from Ellen Wang of the CAAFD (Council of Aspiring American Fashion Designers) to showcase my collection at New York

Fashion Week as an emerging designer. I couldn't believe it but I had to turn it down as participation fees were beyond what I would like to spend," he recalled.

In April 2017, Ellen Wang and her group from CAAFFD wrote Seneriches again to invite him to the September Spring Summer 2018 showcase and for the same reasons, he had to say no since the costs were too rich for him: almost $25,000. Things turned around in July 2017 when Wang offered him 85 percent sponsorship, apparently impressed that he should show his designs at New York Fashion Week.

"On September 10, 2017 I presented my Mikelsen collection at Chelsea Piers in New York, along with four other emerging designers. Seeing my creations on the models in the dressing area was very exciting, and hearing positive comments from staff and different people backstage was also very reassuring," he said.

For him, the reception to his work was surreal. "The most unbelievable feeling came when I walked the long runway with my final model, to shouts and applause from the crowd, flashes from cameras, handshakes, thumbs up, etc. I felt like I was floating in space. My heart and spirit were filled with life. But with that elation came a sense of love and humility, gratitude and great accomplishment- that I can finally say I made it to the top and the beginning of more success," he said emotionally.

Seneriches looks up to some of the great designers in the world like Raf Simmons, Oscar de la Renta, Alber Elbaz, Tom Ford and Christian Dior. He is also hoping to dress up Michelle Obama, Kate Middleton and Angelina Jolie, among others, but quickly added that he'd be glad to dress anyone at the right opportunity and time. He believes that, like any art form, the eyes need only a few elements to get the message and take it to different levels of appreciation.

"I want to just give the basic silhouettes and incorporate it with a few classic design elements. After the New York Fashion Week, I feel like the universe is a gift to all of us who were given the opportunity to be born in this world," he explained, overwhelmed by the honor.

"Beauty has no labels or ethnic backgrounds for me. What you see is what you get." What you see with Michael Seneriches and his work is the Filipino's creative soul at its best.

14

FILIPINA CAREGIVER RISES FROM CRISIS, STRONGER

For immigrants, America can mean many things. For Emily Uy, it's a place for 2nd chances, for reinventing yourself and succeeding, even after facing a new crisis that almost cost her life but emerged stronger.

Emily, 58, fled the Philippines after being victimized by a close family friend, betrayed in a swindle that wiped out her savings. Before that she was a businesswoman and a financial consultant in one of the leading insurance companies back home. She has an accountant's degree. Settling in Eagle Rock on the outskirts of Los Angeles, Ca. she's become an outstanding caregiver that saw her reap more success than even the peak of her career in the Philippines.

"It was not an easy decision but I had to make a choice, come to America to seek out an economic opportunity so I can still take care of my family or stay and struggle with daily expenses," Uy revealed during the Manila Mail's interview.

In 2014 she was chosen as Caregiver of the Year awardee at the First Home Care Rising Summit in California and 2017 Outstanding Caregiver by Angel Connection Services.

She has been a caregiver for 11 years and has taken on some of the most heart wrenching care work for patients with different disabilities and illnesses. Some of her clients include stroke survivors, ALS patients and those in hospice care.

She arrived in the United States in 2007 leaving two kids and her husband in the Philippines. To stay connected with her family and friends in the Philippines, she relied on social media to chat with her love ones or check what's going on with their lives. She also joined a non-profit organization and actively involved herself in different activities.

"Luckily, I didn't have any bad experiences and never struggled for work in the US. I tried to be the best that I could be in what I do. I don't let any inferiority complex rule my life. I say what I feel, good or bad. I have friends who helped me get a job the first time I arrived," she said.

However, in 2009 after being employed as a caregiver for two years Emily had to face the greatest battle of her life. She started having routine mammogram when she turned 48 and for two consecutive years results came out normal until she was diagnosed with breast cancer when she was 50.

"After hearing what the doctor said that I have a malignant stage 1 breast cancer, I totally shut down mentally, not hearing anymore the rest of what the doctor said, I felt numb, I felt like it was going to burst. I was in a state of numbness and disbelief. After reality sunk in, I cried, bawled and wailed like what happens when one hears the word cancer. My family in the Philippines was devastated, very sad and worried about the news. They wanted me to go home so they can take care of me," she recalled with sadness.

The devastating news affected her but with the will to survive and access to the best medical treatment in America she felt she could prevail. No one offered to help her with the medical expenses. "The hospital where I had my mammogram gave me a list of clinics and hospitals to call when I told them I had no money and no health insurance. I called each and every number on the list but almost all didn't offer any financial aid," she explained.

Uy never wavered on her faith in God. She never questioned God why she was afflicted with this dreaded disease. She prayed hard like she has never prayed before and then one day she got a surprise call from a social worker at Harbor UCLA Medical Center in Los Angeles, Ca. asking her to come in for an interview. She talked to the social worker and was lucky to be qualified for medical treatment under the Breast and Cervical Cancer Treatment Program. "I didn't spend a single cent on my treatments and surgeries and medicines. I have the best doctors and facilities. Everything was taken care of by the Medical Center," she said.

Uy underwent two surgeries lumpectomy (removal of cancer cells and its surrounding tissues) and oophorectomy (laparoscopic removal of ovaries), four courses of chemotherapy and 37 sessions of radiation. She believes that God provided everything what her heart desired.

"Had this cancer happened in the Philippines, I would be very worried where to get the money for my treatments. Also, I was in good health despite having cancer. I didn't suffer any side effects especially during months of intensive chemotherapy and radiation. I didn't wallow in self-pity or anger but look at my trials with a happy disposition and happy thoughts," she added.

At the moment Emily is motivated to provide her family in the Philippines a better and more comfortable life. She is also motivated to advocate and be a voice for other caregivers in the United States. Even caregivers need someone to care about them.

15

FIL-AM MARTIAL ARTS 'BLACKBELTER' FINDS HIS PASSION IN MAKING MOVIES THAT MAKE HIM HAPPY

Research technician June Daguiso retired recently after 30 years in the law firm Hogan & Lovells in Washington D.C. But rather than close a chapter in his life, it seems to have widened the doors for his other passion, marrying martial arts with making films.

June, a resident of Culpeper, Va. is a 4th degree black-belter in Taekwondo and 1st degree in Shotokan. He worked for 10 years as an instructor for several karate schools in Northern Virginia.

However, instead of relaxing and spending more time now with his family or travel around the world, he decided to pursue his childhood dream of becoming an actor and a filmmaker.

"I loved watching movies while growing up in Manila; I loved watching Bruce Lee and Kung Fu movies and that led me to learn martial arts, my dream was to be an actor in an action film," he said during the Manila Mail's interview.

Back in 2006, Daguiso was cast as an "extra" (bit role player) with a short speaking part in a horror film "Deadlands", produced and directed by winning director Gary Ugarek. That same year he was hired as a stunt man and fight choreographer for an action drama film.

"I worked very closely with the producer of the film and started learning the process of making an Indie film. I started writing screenplays and taught myself editing my own films. I don't have any preferences in terms of movie genre. I write screenplays based on what comes out of my head. If I had a big budget, I may stick to an action-drama because that is the most appealing to all audiences," he explained.

Daguiso's first feature film "Full Circle" got excellent reviews at Amazon. "It's got all the usual wholesome ingredients. Good story, good fight scene and nice special effects for a low budget film," wrote by Jake Jacobson who purchased the DVD of the movie at Amazon.

Another reviewer by the name of Alexander Tapanya said: "I've watched a lot of Independent films but I've never seen one with such a great story line as this one. If this movie was produced with a Hollywood budget, this one would be a big seller,"

Budget has always been the problem for any movies to be produced but Daguiso was able to connect himself with some groups of talented people in the Washington DC area and found investors willing to put their money in the movie.

"I was just lucky that I have a bunch of talented actors who share my passion and doing it for the love of arts. Making it in the film industry is difficult especially if you don't have the right connection or not in a small circle of Hollywood elites," he said.

Daguiso used his own money and savings for his first five feature films, "Full Circle," "Collide" and the "Drug Related Trilogy."

"I got it all back from screening the films several times and selling DVD's. The rest of my films are funded by several individuals as executive producers who want to be part of my movie projects," he declared.

Presently, Daguiso just finished producing another action film, "Romeo Must Die Again," and another comedy, "Table For Eight," filmed in the Caribbean last year and now he is producing a TV series entitled "Serial Madness".

Running an international film festival is another way for Daguiso to watch all kinds of films and connect with other Indie filmmakers around the world. Now on its 10th year, "The World Music and Independent Film Festival" was started by Daguiso. His mission is not only to add opportunities for DC, Maryland and Virginia Indie filmmakers but also to provide a platform of achievements for international cinema artists.

"It was so hard in the beginning since you need a lot of money to fund the festival. It takes a lot of my time watching hundreds of films submitted every year, then dealing with the nominated artists, and coordinating weeklong festival, and planning on running the gala and awarding in the cruise ship," Daguiso explained.

Finally, when I asked him what's his philosophy in life as a film-maker, he replied "No matter what movie you make, there's always someone who will hate it and criticize your work, so do it to make yourself happy and nothing else matters."

16

REUNION: NEVER FORGOTTEN, A GRANDFATHER RETURNS TO PLACES IN THE HEART

Over the years, Ronie Lumauag Mataquel — a math teacher at John Bowne High School in Flushing, New York — has received numerous awards as an outstanding Filipino teacher and overseas foreign worker in the United States. The 44-year-old native of Initan Sibalom, Antique has been recognized for "Excellence in Education" by Jersey City's PAN-American Concerned Citizens Action League, New York's Team United Maharlika Foundation, Inc., the Garden State Filipino American Association and the

Fil-Am Needs Literacy Program in the Bronx, NY, notably for his "Outstanding Leadership" as President of the United Federation of FilipinoAmerican Educators.

But while Ronie feels greatly honored by these tributes, his most memorable and meaningful award was the achievement of a young man's fervent dream: discovering that his 88-year-old maternal grandfather, Felomino Lumauag, was still alive and hugging him for the first time. It was also the fulfillment of a wish harbored for many years by his 62-year-old mother, Rosemarie Lumauag Mataquel, who never knew her father.

Ronie's grandmother, Matilde Hamco, met Felomino Lumauag when she was in Manila serving as a nanny for his grandfather's aunts. Felomino then left to serve in the U.S. Navy while Matilde was pregnant with Rosemarie, Ronie's mother. But Felomino never came back. Matilde died in 2012 at the age of 77. "After college and while working in Manila, I would spend several afternoons or weekends looking for my grandfather to help my Mom, who never stopped looking for him," Ronie said. "The agony that there was a man out there, who was my mother's biological father, consumed all our energy. The sad part was, you don't have any clue why he didn't find ways to find her. Was he ever aware that he had a child waiting for him?"

Ronie came to the U.S. in 2003 and started teaching in New York. In 2007, while spending one summer vacation in Antique, his grandmother asked him to search for his grandfather's nephews and nieces in the United States. Ronie then went online and decided to dig deeper into his origins. He googled several sites to help him in his search, but to no avail. Eventually, he found someone to undertake a more intensive search for his extended family.

What really motivated Ronie to look for his grandfather was the missing link inside their family. His mother graduated with honors in elementary but could not continue her high school education since his grandmother couldn't afford to send his mother to school. For about 40 to 50 years, his mother continued the search but didn't have the means to do so, other than by pen and paper. Due to unknown addresses, the letters could not be delivered so the returned letters would pile up. To his mother, the earnest search for her father was always on her mind.

Finally, in September 2013, Ronie received some good news. "When I received the report detailing contact information of relatives, I started calling the numbers," he recalls. "I felt blessed when I was able to speak to one of them. On September 12, I found out much to my delight that my grandfather was still alive.

Breaking the news to his family in Antique, especially to his beloved mother, wasn't easy. For seven months, Ronie secretly communicated with his grandfather without informing anyone.

He eventually broke his silence and told his mother on April 2, 2014. "It was a phone call I made on her birthday," he recalls. "It was a very memorable moment when I told my mother the news. For the first time in 58 years, she was talking on the phone with her father. It was so intense. My mom was crying the whole time while my grandfather was asking for forgiveness. I know she was shocked that I found him but we considered it a miracle. During their phone conversation I can vividly remember what he said: 'Now I am ready to leave this world because I got the chance to ask forgiveness from you.' He continued telling my mom that he had a mission to fulfill, and that's the reason he's still alive.

More than a year later, on August 12, 2015, their first family reunion happened in Honolulu, Hawaii. His grandfather and wife, Carmelita Jean Lumauag, are owners of Mabuhay Cafe and Restaurant, the first Filipino restaurant in Honolulu. Ronie brought along his wife, three children and his mother.

"It's a very strange feeling," Ronie recalls the day he met his grandfather. "I can't explain the joy and the excitement that, finally, I had the chance to hug and embrace someone that brought us into this world. Someone I didn't expect to show up even in my wildest dreams but he did. I won't deny the fact that, like my mom, I grew up with resentments but as soon as I saw him I forgot everything and I accepted him wholeheartedly."

Ronie remembers his mother literally shaking with excitement and nervousness when she met his father for the first time. "Tears streamed down her face after their first hug. She had never been happier in her whole life," he said.

Understandably, there was tension between his mother and grandfather during their first encounter. But after awhile, Ronie said, the two were sweetly talking to each other. That's when the pain of separation, deepened even more by time and space, slowly began to disappear.

At the family reunion, true love and harmony reigned. There were places in the heart that welcomed Ronie's grandfather back into their lives.

17

PINAY 'BABY WHISPERER' SPREADS CARE FOR PARENTS, INFANTS ALIKE

Filipinas are known to be among the most nurturing and reliable caregivers- qualities that have helped a former beauty queen and accountant carve a niche as a "baby whisperer" in New York.

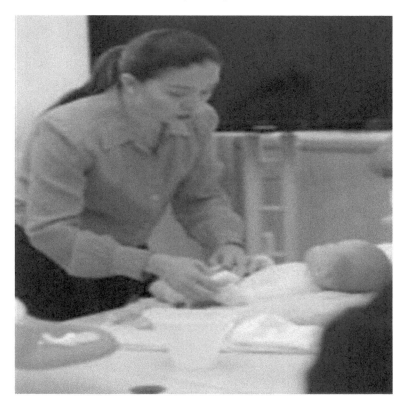

Ruby Abangan Sibal, 40, earned her accounting degree in 1996 at the University of San Agustin in Iloilo City. The local beauty queen later worked as a ground stewardess and advertising agent for Philippine Airlines. She's now one of the most-sought after Newborn Care Specialist or "Baby Nurse" across the United States.

She's been called a "Mary Poppins" and "Baby Whisperer" but her primary role today is being the CEO of Beyond Baby Care, LLC which she formed in New York City in 2015. "I told myself, why not build a business? I did some research and registered my business and I found out it was not that hard. I am now an independent contractor and I'm hiring people," Ruby revealed.

When she immigrated to America in 2011, she wanted to pursue her dream of being a floral designer. After all, her family in Iloilo had a thriving flower shop business. But she soon realized that pursuing her interest in floral design was tough and financially challenging. While trying to establish her life as an immigrant and away from her two kids (now 14 and 11 years old), she tried all kinds of jobs - as caregiver, housekeeper home-call masseuse, event organizer, make-up artist, babysitter and nanny.

Then in one defining moment, while working as a babysitter, a friend introduced her to baby nursing. Ruby realized then that she had a natural way of calming babies to sleep. She decided to enroll for online classes for infant care, and her credentials now include Newborn Care Expert, Certified Infant Massage Instructor and Certified Lactation Educator Counselor and Certified Educator of Happiest Baby On The Block, giving her incredible experience as a Newborn Care Specialist.

Dr. Harvey Karp, the author of the best-selling book "Happiest Baby on the Block" is also Ruby's mentor and biggest supporter. "Babies are so innocent and it is just so fulfilling to be a part of child's life that's why I decided to become a Newborn Care Specialist," she averred.

"It's also challenging due to lack of sleep because my job requires 24-hour shifts but I told myself, I will make this my profession," Ruby explained in an interview for the Manila Mail and for radio show "Pilipinas sa Amerika."

Ruby admitted that when she was a first-time mom, she was scared to give her own baby a bath until the age of three months. "Now I can take care of twin babies, give them a bath at the same time without feeling scared. I learned to love my job not because it is all about taking care of babies but it's basically coaching the parents as well by trying to navigate the proper way of infant care from sleep, swaddling, feeding and other aspects of an infant's development."

Ruby doesn't have any nursing background but pediatricians, first-time parents, women who have delicate pregnancies or C-sections are booking her in advance because of her expertise. Even experienced parents hire her so moms can recover from delivery and devote their time to their other children. She usually takes care of an infant until the age of three months.

She's became so popular she had to turn down some clients. She's been mentioned in such popular baby care websites as Mamaviews.com. One client named Katie Ullman wrote "Ruby Sibal is truly the Mary Poppins of baby nurses - the absolute BEST! Ruby not only met, but far exceeded my expectations in every way possible and did many things far beyond the realm of a typical baby nurse. She kept a meticulously detailed baby journal. She taught us several things to look out, massage and techniques to treat infant gas which can cause much infant discomfort. Another client wrote "My sister calls Ruby "The Baby Whisperer," and I agree! As her name suggests, she is a definite gem indeed."

Ruby's biggest goal as a Newborn Care Specialist is to share her expertise with others who would like to follow her footsteps and success. "I have students that after I trained them, the next day they also got a job from me because I can vouch for them. I refer them to some of my clients whenever I'm not available. The most important thing is training and experience. If my clients learned that I trained and mentor a prospective baby nurse, usually they get hired which makes me very happy because I felt like I was also hired."

18

LIFE OF HARDSHIP FINALLY PAYS OFF FOR PINOY MENTOR IN NY

Ernesto Pamolarco, Jr. came to America for an international conference in 2005 and decided to stay; he worked the system, pursuing a Master's degree in New York, washing dishes, cleaning homes until he got a visa to legally live and work in the United States. He has since won accolades as a special education teacher and recently recognized by the Office of New York City Comptroller, Pan American Concerned Citizens Action League and the Association of Filipino Teachers.

After arriving for a conference in Michigan, he applied for a six-month extension of his tourist visa and requested the USCIS to convert it to a student visa through the help of a Filipino professor in New York City.

The professor helped him enroll and continue his Master's Degree in Early Childhood and Special Education. To support his life in New York and family in the Philippines. Ernesto worked as a dishwasher for a Filipino restaurant, housekeeper in a mansion with 21 rooms to clean every day and other menial jobs to make ends meet.

His diligence and determination were rewarded when he was offered a job to become a manager for a private physical therapy clinic in Brooklyn, New York. He received a working visa with the help of the owner's sponsorship letter. He was also able to petition his family from the Philippines.

Ernesto was the 6th of seven children of Ernesto Pamolarco Sr. and Pacita Serdena of Jubav, Culubian, Leyte. He was the only one in the family who finished college and received a Master's degree. "Most of the time we ate crops and corn because we couldn't afford to buy rice. I also experienced having salt as viand paired with rice and got used to sleeping on an empty stomach," he recalled.

At the age nine, his father was stabbed to death by a neighbor during a village feast. His mother remarried a man who turned out to be a drunkard and who once threatened to cut off his fingers when there was no food to eat. He decided to leave Leyte and find his future in Manila.

At the age of 13, he ended up working as dishwasher at a Chinese restaurant along Recto Ave., Manila and also sold plastic wrappers. He decided that school in Leyte offered more prospects than being a street kid in Manila, he went back home to pursue his studies in high school.

For college, he went to Naval State University in Naval, Biliran, attending evening classes, while working as a baker, tricycle driver, karaoke bar operator and other jobs during the day. It was a constant and necessary effort to support himself and fulfill his ambition to become a teacher. When he started looking for a teaching job, he ended up working as a janitor because he didn't have a license in teaching.

"I befriended the teachers and learned from them how to take the Philippine Board Examination for Teachers and the first time I passed it," he said proudly.

"I am a very persevering and a persistent person. I know that I have to start from the bottom. It didn't bother me at all doing those odd and hard jobs. I know that someday if I work hard, I will get the kind of job which fits for my education and qualification and experiences. If I don't get it, at least I tried and maybe God had another plan for me. I am not easily discouraged by hardships or trials. I take them as opportunities for me to test my own limits," Ernesto explained. He is currently the Chairman of the Board of Youth Success Global Foundation. Inc., a non-profit organization in New York that helps students with learning disabilities.

"As a Special Education Teacher, I have to handle children with special needs with special care. Although they have different issues and concerns, I believe that they are unique individuals capable of learning at their own pace and style. They are like plants. Some plants need more water and some don't. Some don't need too much exposure to sunlight while others need sunlight to survive," he said. Ernesto is now happy with his life as a successful Filipino immigrant. He never thought he would reach this far in life.

"God gave me more than what I need in life. I feel that success as a Filipino immigrant means to live happily with my family and friends in the community. I intend to retire in the Philippines. If I still have the energy I will teach in colleges and universities in Manila or maybe in my alma matter or continue my new passion, farming and gardening," he declared.

19

ABANDONED AT BIRTH, FIL-AM WORK HIS WAY TO TOP

Abandoned by his American father, Richard Holsman struggled to eke a living in Southern Leyte, a backwater eastern province that lies along the Philippine's "typhoon highway"

From that humble beginning, Holsman, now 41, is the CEO and President of Holsman Physical Therapy and Rehabilitation Centers that operates in New Jersey and New York.

To this day, he is at a loss on how his biological father, a businessman from Hawaii, met his mother in the Philippines. "My biological father didn't even know if I was born. I grew up not getting any support from him. I have not known or seen him," he said sadly in an interview with the Manila Mail.

Holsman grew up independent and mostly in the care of a grandmother in Southern Leyte. His mother remarried an Englishman. They lived and worked in England and Papua New Guinea. They supported him along the way with his Aunt Josephine in Makati part of the Metro Manila capital region. He has one sister and two brothers.

"After graduating from high school and up to my third year in college, I was selling vegetables at a wet market (palengke) in Alabang and Muntinlupa selling onions, tomatoes, cabbage and etc. The values of hard work, fear of God and the determination to succeed were instilled in me at a young age by my grandmother. I was able to experience seeing her barbecue fish or do the "tinapa' in the wee hours of the morning and sell it during the day," he said.

For Holsman, coming to America was not an easy journey. The path for him was the US Physical Therapy Examination in 1998, facilitated by a New York-based employer, after graduating with Bachelor of Science in Physical Therapy degree from the University of Perpetual Help in Rizal.

This was quickly followed by a Masters of Arts in Teaching Major and Health Education.

He was lucky to be one of the applicants selected out of 250. He got his US work on September 28, 2001 and arrived in a traumatized America, and a devastated New York City.

He was assigned to three different worksites in New York City days after he arrived. He would work for four days a week as a School Physical Therapist in the morning and then work in an out-patient setting in the afternoon and the evening in Manhattan; and one day a week in Queens. After six months, he was transferred to New Jersey in a Sub-Acute Rehab Nursing Facility (Forest Hill Healthcare Center) where he worked for 11 years as a Staff Physical Therapist, Assistant Director of Rehab, Director of Rehab and Director of Quality Assurance. While working at Forest Hill five days a week, he managed to earn a specialty certification in Geriatric Physical Therapy.

In 2004, he started building the Holsman Healthcare, LLC, a healthcare staffing and consulting company. The following year, he started building the Home Therapy LLC that provides Physical Therapy services to patients in their homes. Finally, in 2011, he founded the Holsman Physical Therapy and Rehabilitation PC- a clinic group practice manned by physical therapists, occupational therapists and speech therapists as well as chiropractors and massage therapists. The Holsman group of companies currently employs over 75 employees; and owns and operates 15 outpatient Rehabilitation Centers in New Jersey and New York City.

In addition, he was able to finish a degree at Boston University Sargent College of Health and Rehabilitation Sciences in 2013.

"I always dreamed of opening a company in the UnitedStates even when I was in the Philippines, so it was just a matter of time and capital that I would eventually put up my own business," he averred.

"When I first started working in the US, I was working 12 hours a day, seven days a week when a typical PT would work only eight hours a day, 5 days a week. I was working in the hospitals, nursing homes and home care agencies after my full-time job. I had so much work available that I had to start hiring therapists to fill the needs of the employers that wanted my services. I was able to help my patients and at the same time able to help our countrymen by petitioning Physical and Occupational Therapists on a green card or on a working visa at Holsman Healthcare's expense without any cost from the employee," he explained.

"If other people can do it, I certainly can do it," Holsman declared.

"Never give up and don't be afraid to ask for help when needed. Always put God and people first," he beamed with the quiet aura of a man who's crossed an ocean and found success on the other side.

20

FILIPINO EDUCATOR HAILED FOR INNOVATIVE TEACHING METHOD

Rolan Gutierrez Photography

MOST people dislike Mathematics. Some find it boring and difficult to understand but for a Filipino Math Teacher like Ramil Buenaventura, 47, who lives with his wife and two kids in Queens, New York instilling a love of learning and fostering creativity while teaching Math is important to make it more fun, awesome and enjoyable for his students. He is now known in the United States as the Singing-Dancing Math Teacher, Math YouTuber and a Representative of Outstanding Teachers in his field because of his passionate attitude and hardworking craft as a teacher. He teaches 7th and 8th grade students at the Renaissance Charter School in Jackson Heights, New York.

Before emigrating to the US, Ramil was a middle school math teacher of La Salle Greenhills in Mandaluyong City, Manila. He was working for 13 years as a teacher when there was a shortage of teachers in America and the Department of Education in New York City went to the Philippines and hired hundreds of teachers and he was one of the luckiest teachers to apply.

"Going to America was not really my dream back then but I tried and I was lucky to be hired in 2003. By God's grace, it was a gift from the Lord," Ramil explained during my interview for MANILA MAIL and for my radio show "Pilipinas sa Amerika."

Ramil was given H1B Visa and everything went smoothly after paying $6K to a recruitment agency who hired him in the Philippines. He had to borrow some money from friends and families just to be able to come to the US.

Ramil grew up in Mandaluyong and studied in Don Bosco for Elementary and High School. He was an ex- seminarian and his first ambition was to be a priest. He studied Education major in Math at Jose Rizal University, Mandaluyong City and graduated Cum Laude.

He got his Master's Degree in Education, Major in Educational Technology at the University of the Philippines in Diliman, Quezon City.

When Ramil arrived in America, he experienced a culture shock in dealing with his students. "Ang pinakaluko-lukong bata or pasaway na bata sa Pilipinas is just an ordinary kid in America. My 13 years of experience in being a teacher is not just zero but I go back to negative."

Ramil has to learn everything again the language, culture, and he encountered so many challenges during the first few months, he started teaching in New York. He was sent to the most challenging neighborhoods of New York City where American teachers gave up teaching the kids.

"Almost 170 Filipino teachers *kasama na ako ang kinalat sa* New York City just to teach kids. The kids don't call me Sir but Mr. B; and they couldn't understand at times my Filipino accent. *Ang English natin sa Pilipinas parang formal English pero 'di nila maintindihan. Noong bago ako,* "Oh, take out your ballpen! Pen pala; 'di mo dapat sabihing 'ballpen.' Bring out your bond paper or coupon bond; no, it's a white paper. Line up in the corridor, where's the corridor? *Sabi nila.* No, it's the hallway. Do you wanna go to the comfort room? It's not a comfort room, it's a restroom. When I talked to the school principal. I told her, I don't know why I come to this country. I tried everything to be strict, they laughed at me. I tried to be gentle with them they still laughed at me," Ramil said.

He wasn't the only teacher who experienced bullying and insults from their students but other Filipino teachers as well. Some got sick because of pressure and depression at work. Of course, Ramil was able to survive the challenges by the help of a mentor and learning about classroom management by attending various educational and leadership oriented professional development.

"In America I learned to grow as a teacher *at natuto sa aking mistakes.* I put myself in the shoes of my students. I show my students how creative I am. *Kung nasa classroom ako, ayoko ng boring at walang kabuhay-buhay na libro-libro lang, because of technology kailangang iangat mo rin iyong level mo. Kasi ang competition mo dito, social media, computer, TV at tapos iyong teacher sa harap boring na nagsasalita walang impact kaya kailangang lalabanan ko. I tried to upgrade myself then mag-aaral ako, gagaya sa YouTube kung anong nakikita ko.* If you see something good, take it, use it *at kung hindi umobra* it's another one," Ramil told the MANILA MAIL.

In Ramil's classroom you will see him dancing, rapping and dancing on the tables and uses game applications. He even made a music video all about mathematics just to grab his students attention. His sessions normally start with a little lecture but he makes sure his students are continually engaged by adding a little game where they can apply the math skills they have learned. Students get extra points for participating in the games.

Through his talent in singing, dancing and making videos while teaching Math he developed math and educational videos which are easily accessible to students and his colleagues. As testament to his innovation are the various awards and citations he received. Some of these include an award of the Hometown Heroes selected by NEW YORK DAILY NEWS, 2014 Big Apple Awardee for Teacher's Excellence, Outstanding OFW Award in Education (2016), Ulirang Guro Award, Outstanding Filipino Catholic Award.

"Teach minds, touch hearts, inspire hands. I want to build a relationship of trust with my students. Only then will they feel safe and secure in the teaching-learning environment in my class. Teaching should be purposeful and there should be fun and excitement in the process. Learning should be multifaceted. The more senses are involved in learning something, the more it becomes part of one's being," Ramil explained with the pure passion of a true math teacher that everyone can count on.

21

BRUNSWICK'S 1ST EVER FIL-AM MAYOR EYES 2ND TERM

Ohio's 1st Filipino-American Mayor Ron Falconi, 48, has been interested in politics from a young age, growing up in Brunswick, he admitted feeling alienated, suffering through racial discrimination. He saw public service and politics as a way to shake them off by making real change.

He's volunteered for a wide variety of Republican Party campaigns ranging from city council all the way to U.S. President.

"About ten years ago, I decided to run on the ballot myself. Although I lost in my first try, I eventually became an elected official," he explained.

This coming January 2018, I will have been in elected office for ten years in the City of Brunswick (Councilman 2009-2013, Mayor 2014-present). I did lose my first election in 2007 by 141 votes. That was disappointing. However, I was able to put that behind me and go forward," he told the Manila Mail.

"Mayor Falconi was born and raised in Cleveland, Ohio. He is an immigration lawyer by profession. He is married to Genevive Cachuela Falconi, Section Head of Pediatrics at the Cleveland Clinic in Brunswick. She is the daughter of the late Muntinlupa City Councilman Ernesto Cachuela. They have two kids, Joey and Angela, who are both in high school.

Mayor Falconi is the son of Filipino immigrants who came to the United States in the 1960's. His father, now deceased, Edgardo Falconi was an electrical engineer and his mother Teresita Liongson from Manila was a physician.

"My parents met at the U.S. Embassy in Manila. They were both applying for a visa to come into the U.S. and they both wanted to find a new life in America. First, they settled in Los Angeles then moved to Cleveland, Ohio for better opportunities. I have one sister named Lourdes who's an Ob/Gyn and lives in Ohio."

Mayor Falconi shared that while growing up he experienced feeling like an outsider. He and his sister experienced racial discrimination and some people assumed that they were foreigners. "As Filipinos, we were the minority of the minority in Brunswick. It is a city of 35,000 people and the people are mostly whites, not a large Filipino community and almost everyone know each other. I knew that we did not look like everybody else, but it didn't prohibit me from moving forward in life and treat other people with respect."

"As a father, the city leader said he teaches his kids about the value of hard work, diligence, and a close relationship with God. He believes as long as you work hard, good things will happen to you."

Mayor Falconi feels good that in the upcoming November 2017 election in Brunswick, he will have no opponent. He thinks that all elected officials, whether they are from the Philippines or from the United States, should always remember that they are there to serve their constituents.

"Public officials serve the public- NOT the other way around. Having a title does not really mean anything. It is what you do with the leadership that counts. I want to be remembered as someone who made the City of Brunswick a better place than it was when I first came to city hall 10 years ago. As the son of two immigrants who came to this country in 1960's, it is humbling to be one of the only Filipino-American Mayors in the country today. I hope that number increases as the time passes by," he explained.

During the 2016 Presidential Campaign, Mayor Falconi was selected by Donald Trump to be one of the leading voices in the Asian American Pacific Islander Advisory Committee.

He was also one of two Fil-Am leaders from across the US selected by the Japanese government to participate in the Kakehashi Project for Asian American Leadership. (Kakehashi means bridge in Japanese).

On plans to run for higher office in the future, he humbly answers with political prudence. "Right now, I'm excited to continue to serve the people of Brunswick, Ohio. I look forward to my second term."

22

FIL-AM NURSE WEARS CHARITY, SERVICE, AS BADGE OF HONOR

Nurse Leolalinda Petinglay Plameras, 48, has demonstrated that out of poverty springs great compassion. Growing up in a remote village of Antique province in the Central Philippine island of Panay, she was recently awarded the Frist Humanitarian Award, the highest honor given by the Hospital Corporation of America to employees, physicians, caregivers and volunteers who provide their patients with excellent care and service to the community.

Her parents were both elementary teachers and she's the 10th child of twelve children. She was taught in the love, mercy and knowledge of God and was raised to give back. Her grandparents were devout convention Baptist believers who donated a parcel of land on which to build the community's church.

In 2004, she ran for Mayor and almost won over the political dynasty that ruled Antique. Her husband Erwin Plameras is the son of former Antique Governor Jovito Plameras Jr. and they have a 12-year old daughter. She works as a Registered Supervisor in Anchor Rehab and Healthcare of Aiken on 12-hour shifts for two days, and as Doctor's Hospital of Augusta ICU Staff RN for four days. She's also performing a fellowship at her Pastor's house and nursing home; the remaining one day she spends with her family and the Agape Ministry.

"I operate in faith, not expecting but trusting Him as the source of everything. My prayer that God will sustain me physically, mentally, morally and spiritually," she declared.

Because of her compassion and service to those in need, Plameras was recently awarded the Frist Humanitarian Award. The Frist Humanitarian Award was established in 1971 in honor of one of Hospital Corporation of America's s co-founder Dr. Thomas F. Frist Sr. It includes a $5,000 donation to the charity of the recipient's choice and $5,000 for the employee or volunteer.

On Aug. 3, 2016 Plameras founded the Agape Children and Christian Ministries Inc. "I named it Agape because of unconditional and highest love for Jesus that moved me to minister," she explained. The recipients of Agape are less privileged children, teenage girls and boys, young mothers and grandparents. It has several programs like after school, housing program and home ownership for less privileged and homeless, senior citizens boarding home and the international missionary program.

Plameras is a Filipino-American Intensive Care Unit nurse from Aiken, South Carolina. She hails from San Remigio, Antique at the foot of the mountains far from malls and trappings of consumerism. As a young child, there was no cake or ice cream on birthdays. It was a tough and harsh life, she recalled, but she was satisfied in her belief of the presence of God.

On Aug. 23, 2016, Plameras purchased a house in Crosland Park that was riddled with 20 bullets. Almost everyone warned her not to buy the house because of the crimes and violence in the neighborhood but she didn't pay heed.

She trusts her instinct and big faith in God. "Teenagers (boys from 15-18) when starting Agape were wearing their hoods and will not face the camera, didn't want to be touched. One day they broke in the back door of Agape and splattered hundreds to thousands of pieces of broken glasses just to find out, they stole all chocolates in the refrigerator, no other missing items....in other words they were hungry! Instead of getting scared, angry or giving up, I looked down at the broken glasses and cried and asked the

Lord, "if these broken glasses are the broken lives of these teenagers, then so help me God if this is what you want me to tender, I'll commit my strength to you, please protect me, Father as I take care of them."

She continued, "then I started visiting them more often and bringing them food and they started coming and I befriended the neighborhood. Right now, no hoodies, their chin up, they wear the Agape T-shirt and I will continue to mentor them," she told the Manila Mail.

Ms. Plameras added that she is sharing her good deeds definitely not to raise herself but testifying the faithfulness of God and encouraging others who have a little extra or have more to remember the needy especially the homeless and unable to send their children to school.

In the Philippines, she's also doing the same ministry with the help of her husband and other family members. "God showed His power by allowing me to win this 45th Frist Humanitarian Award. Masarap pakinggan na ganito ang nangyari na nakatanggap ka ng award but I would like to be more just like a regular person and still mingle and able to do the work of God. I don't want to be put into a higher place because of the award. I want God to cover me with humility as I continue to serve the children in Agape Minstry," Plameras said, firm in her belief that charitable works are the only way to live a life of fulfillment.

23

THE SECRETS OF LOLO CELESTINO ALMEDA

Lolo Celestino Almeda has been in the news for the Filipino community in the Metro DC region because of his contributions during World War II and the fight for recognition for his comrades. He recently turned 100. Humanity, he says, will always have its wars and upheavals but he counsels to anyone who'd care to listen, "always look at the brighter side of life".

As one of the remaining surviving veterans of the Pacific War, Lolo Celestino continues to hope that the United States government would eventually recognize his military service and give him the $15,000 "equity compensation" promised them. The sum goes beyond mere compensation. It is also about justice for thousands of Filipinos who served under the American flag, in defense of American liberty and security, who lived through the horrors of war but died without their toils and sacrifices recognized.

For now, Lolo Celestino is looking forward to receiving the US Congressional Gold Medal Award from House Speaker Paul Ryan, along with other Filipino WW2 veterans. It is something that holds a special place in his heart. When I interviewed him, I was very impressed by the sharpness of his mind in remembering dates, names of people, facts and events. Many people regardless of their stature in life have asked him about his secret to longevity.

To this he responded. "No women, wine nor song. I do not have a secret for longevity. In the poem Sohrab and Rustum, it says our fate is written in heaven at the same time at birth," he explained during the Manila Mail interview.

Lolo Celestino was a high school vocational arts instructor in the Philippines before the World War II broke out. The Philippines was then a Commonwealth Territory of the United States. When the war started, he was in the ROTC Reserve Officers Training Corps and was inducted into active duty to the Anti-Sabotage regiment of the Philippine Commonwealth Army.

Born in Binan, Laguna, south of the capital, on June 8, 1917, he emigrated to the U.S. in 1996 with his family. When he was young, he rode a bike or walked to school because his parents couldn't afford to pay his commute.

"We were very poor, I would walk miles and miles to school and to work. We couldn't afford junk food, meat and all the trendy foods that were sold at that time. We ate vegetables that my parents grew in our backyard. Little did we know, that this is the healthiest food for our body," he said.

Today, it takes an hour for Lolo Celestino to walk the three blocks around his neighborhood in Gaithersburg, Maryland. He consumes a half cup of rice for every meal, with fish and vegetables.
Once in a while during the weekends, he eats meat.

"I am very partial to everything "paksiw"- paksiw na pata, paksiw na isda, leche flan, lechon kawali, chicharon and his favorite bopis and dinuguan"

In addition, he likes doing little things at home but lately his eye sight has been hindering his ability to do the things he loved, like gardening, carpentry and fixing cars. According to Lolo Celestino, he never had a problem with his cholesterol level or blood pressure. He is the youngest of the five children. His mother died at the age of 40 because of blood poisoning when she got injured with a scrap metal; his father died at the age of 78. To exercise his brain, he reads the Reader's Digest, American Legion Newspaper and Time Magazine. He spends most of his time during the day watching the news on CNN and the Filipino Channel TFC.

"Hindi ko naramdamang 100 years old na ako (I don't feel I'm already 100), I feel like I'm only 65 years old. Age is just a number," he said. Lolo Celestino believes in the golden rule "Do unto others as you would have them do unto you." His life's philosophy is "There is nothing perfect in this world. The earth has its highest mountains and deepest waters. Humanity has war, revolution and doubts but always look at the brighter side of life. If I can't say anything good to anyone,
I shut up." We should all feel good that these days, at 100 years old, Lolo Celestino still has a lot to offer for anyone who's wise enough to listen.

24

FIL-AM CLIMBS OUT OF POVERTY TO BECOME ACE NY LAWYER

"Poverty is a source of motivation in itself," says Filipino American lawyer Nicholas "Nick" Caraquel, adding "You can become creative in finding ways to get out of that poverty."

For Caraquel, 44, now a much-in-demand lawyer based in Elmhurst, New York, t's been a long hard climb from "banana cue" (fried sugar-coated banana) vendor in the streets of San Isidro, Davao Oriental. A run-in with airport authorities when he first visited the United States convinced him to focus on immigration law.

"I focus on immigration law because it's my passion to help other people and immigration is an area where I can greatly demonstrate that," he explained.

He was held for two hours by immigration officers when he first visited the U.S. "They grilled me. They thought I will become a "TNT" (undocumented immigrant) and that experience put me now in a better position to give specific advice to my Kababayans" Nick explained.

But it was an arduous journey from Mindanao to the shadows of Manhattan. The 6th of seven children, his father was a barber while his mother was a seamstress. "My Mom Grade 1 lang ang natapos, my Dad naman Grade 3 or Grade 4 lang ang natapos. He doesn't believe in education. Kasi sa kanya, kahit ano pa ang natapos mo, you have to do what you need to do to survive on a day to day basis. Iyong Nanay ko naman iba siya, gusto niyang makatapos kami ng pag-aaral kasi ayaw n'yang maranasan namin ang paghihirap." Nick explained, comparing the priorities of his parents.

Because of the financial needs of his older siblings who were in school, his parents asked him to quit schooling and help his mom by selling banana cue in a bus terminal. He was always around for her and his younger sister. He stopped school for a year after completing Grade 3.

"I could not understand the reason why I needed to stop going to school. I was mad, bakit ako ang pinili n'yo na huminto at magbenta ng saging? Eh, nasa special class ako. Papayag lang ako na magbenta ng saging kapag one-year lang ang kontrata natin." (I was mad, I was asking why I had to be the one to quit school to sell bananas? I was in special class. I agreed only with the understanding I would do it for one year)

It took six months for Nick to fully understand why he wasn't in school anymore and accept everything. But he learned the value of hard work, determination, patience, being prayerful, and never give up on your dreams. When Nick finished High School, he was selected for the State Scholarship Program of Davao Oriental where he was given the opportunity to study in Ateneo de Davao University.

He pursued a degree in Bachelor of Science in Industrial Engineering. His mom got very sick in his last three years in college. Their small store was also demolished due to a road widening project and had to rely on his father's P100 (about $2) daily income from his barbershop with seven children. Nick said he skipped meals for days on end.

"I slept on an empty stomach on my birthday. Life was not easy then," he recounted. "Ang hirap maging mahirap" (It's tough to be poor).

College became his best route out of poverty. When Nick got a job after college his dream of becoming a lawyer did not go away. When he was able to save some money, he decided to enroll at the Xavier University law school.

In 2007, he vacationed in Seattle, Washington. "Originally, I didn't plan going to America, because if you are poor going to America is a far-fetched dream but later in my life I realized when God really wants you to be in some place, He will find a way."

Just three weeks after Nick's arrival in the U.S. he was hired by Nestle Philippines to head their industrial engineering department in Kentucky. However, in encounters with Filipinos they would seek advice from him about immigration. It inspired and encouraged him to find ways on how to be a practicing lawyer in America.

Thanks to a promotion, Nestle moved him to New Jersey. There he learned that New York State allows foreign lawyers to take the bar exam without going back to law school again. In 2012 Nick passed the New York

State Bar Exams and today he is one of the most sought-after immigration lawyers in Elmhurst, New York.

Nick continues to help the poor. He gives school supplies to poor children in their barrio and food for the elderly in the city of Davao Oriental. He's been doing this for the last 15 years and plans to retire in the Philippines for him "there's no place like home."

25

GRAMMY AWARD WINNER TRACES 'IMPOSSIBLE JOURNEY' FROM PH SLUM

Jhett Tolentino and I are Ilonggos who both grew up in the slums of Iloilo City, and shared not only mutual friends but also the "American Dream". The three-time Tony winner annexed last Feb. 12 the Grammy Award for "Best Musical Theater Album".

He won the Grammy for his work on "The Color Purple", a Broadway musical based on Alice Walker's telling of an African - American woman living in America's south in the mid-20th century.

Jhett guested on my radio program "Pilipinas sa Amerika" aired on RMN Iloilo earlier this month. We had a fascinating conversation about that taking home the Grammy Award. It was unexpected, he recalled, and an impossible dream fulfilled with pride and honor.

It was in 1991 during his high school days when he was first made aware of Broadway after his teacher asked in a pop quiz, "Who is the first Filipino to win a Tony Award?". Of course, everyone knew it was Lea Salonga though some in the remote areas didn't know exactly what Broadway was.

He was raised by his beautician mother who died in 2008 and a father who helped provide for the family working as a jeepney driver – a trade he keeps to this day in Iloilo City. He was the youngest of four children but even then was a breadwinner for the family.

In college, Jhett wanted to study Tourism hoping he could be a flight attendant and would be able to travel around the world but the course wasn't offered at the time in Iloilo so he took a scholarship and finished a degree in Accountancy at the University of Iloilo.

In September 2002, he journeyed to California to find a job in sales and marketing but another opportunity came in 2004 to explore the Big

Apple. During the day, he worked as a waiter, grocery bagger, grocery bagger, baby sitter, caregiver and personal assistant.

He did everything to survive on his own but at the end of the day he would find himself lonely and alone without the company of friends and families. To ease the boredom of loneliness, he found himself almost every night watching the Broadway shows

He noticed that almost all the shows were not perfectly crafted. He started a blog "It's All About The Theater" in 2008. Some viewers and performers became aware of his criticisms and then he got his first big break

after the Broadway Press picked up his reviews and invited him for theater presentations.

There he met his producing partner Joan Raffe and they decided to create the JoanJhett Productions which became successful because of their critically acclaimed productions.

He's won Tony Awards for Best Play ("Vanya and Sonia and Masha and Spike," 2013), Best Musical ("A Gentleman's Guide to Love and Murder," 2014), and Best Revival of a Play ("A Raisin in the Sun", 2014).

He's worked with Hollywood stars including Ricky Martin, Glenn Close, Jennifer Hudson, Hugh Jackman, Nick Jonas, Oprah Winfrey and Denzel Washington.

"Life surprised me by being a Tony and Grammy winner but I also believe that everything happens for a reason, not just a blessing in disguise," he said.

At the moment, Jhett is trying to complete and wrap up a documentary, "Life Is What We Make It," aiming for the International Film Festival. The film is a snapshot of his life, how he grew up in the squatter's area of Iloilo City and ended up in Broadway. One of his fondest dreams is to bring Philippine shows to Broadway – a dream that for someone like Jhett Tolentino is within reach. Talent and luck can take you far, and can move you fast in America.

Note: Jhett's film "Life is What We Make It" was released in 2017 and has won several awards in the International Film Festival, including the Australian Independent Film Festival, San Jose International Film Awards, South Film and Arts Academy Festival, 8th Mumbai Shorts International Film Festival, 9Filmfest and Five Continents International Film Festival.

26

THE 'TINY GIRL WITH THE BIG VOICE' WOWS US AUDIENCES

Hollywood is once again moved by the powerful and amazing voice of a Filipino-American – 16 -year-old Anatalia Villaranda, who's wowed audiences of the top-rating singing tilt "The Voice" and whose "lolo" worked in the White House for three American Presidents.

The first time I watched Anatalia on YouTube singing Bruno Mars' "Runaway Baby" I had no doubt that she could be the winner. The tiny girl with a "big voice," as Alicia Keys remarked, received a four-chair turn from celebrity judges Keys, Gwen Stefani, Blake Sheldon and Adam Levine.

All four wanted Anatalia to be in their team but in the end, she chose Keys, explaining they had a good "soul vibe."

I was very interested in knowing the background of Anatalia. It was not an easy interview to do since I had to go through a formal request process. She signed a contract with the NBC that required their permission for press interviews. I also discovered that Anatalia's mother Lea De LaPaz Villaranda is an Ilongga.

Anatalia, was born in Tenecula, California from Filipino parents; her mom is from Bacolod City and her father is from Cagayan de Oro, the pearl city of Northeastern Mindanao. She's the middle child of the three children. Her grandfather on the mother side, Vicente G. Villaranda worked in the White House for 23 years as a valet for Presidents Lyndon Johnson, Richard Nixon and Gerald Ford.

Anatalia started singing at the age of 10, telling her mom one day that she needed to try something new and different as a kid by joining a singing competition. Nobody sang in their family and though Lea was hesitant to let Anatalia join the singing competition, she decided to support her daughter's request. Out of 600 kids, Anatalia was able to make it into the top 30 and capped with a 1st prize finish. It was then Lea realized that her daughter was serious with singing, so she hired a voice coach.

When she was 11, she became part of the group Five Little Princess and they participated in the Nickelodeon Summer Tours. She also appeared on the Disney Channel show "Shake it Up" and on the "Friends for Change" TV commercial. She was briefly taken under the wings of Britney Spears' talent agency. Anatalia also joined the season 15 of American Idol and almost made it to the final round.

According to Lea, she wouldn't have pushed her daughter into singing if she didn't have the talent. "Anatalia sacrificed a lot and work so hard to reach her goal. She is different from other teenagers like her age. She doesn't go out for parties. She just loves line dancing with the elderly people and practice singing every day. She has no boyfriend at all," said her mom with great pride.

"She wants to concentrate on her singing career first and she always told me that boyfriends can always wait."

"As a mom, I always tell her to be respectful with the elders and to other people. I'm so happy that she's such a good, loving and respectful daughter, she helps in the household chores." She confided that before this interview, Anatalia was mowing the lawn and cleaning their house.

For Anatalia, joining the "The Voice USA" and being a crowd favorite was once in a lifetime opportunity. "It's a lot of fun and I didn't expect that I will have four turners in the judges. Everything is surreal and I can't believe I'm on 'The Voice' I was more excited than nervous. I saw Beyonce on stage and I can't wait to see my favorite Bruno Mars as well. I know every single one of his songs and I hope to meet him one day and watch his concert. I chose to go by singing the 'Runaway Baby' during the blind audition because I'm very comfortable singing it, the song is very energetic, upbeat and it really spoke to me."

For the meantime, Anatalia said she wants to have fun and wants to be sure she leaves the stage with no regrets. "I don't even have any special diet for my vocal cords although I really have to start watching what I'm eating and drinking to preserve my voice."

In her interview with the Manila Mail, she revealed that she eats Halo-Halo almost every day and chocolate chip cookies. She also loves her mom's "sinigang na baboy" or sinigang na isda."

For her part, Lea advises her daughter to finish her studies. Anatalia is home schooled and will be graduating from high school this year. Lea says her daughter needs to have fun and enjoy her passion in singing. "If you don't have fun and if you don't have passion into what you are doing, you won't be happy at all" is her mom's advice.

I asked Anatalia what was the first thing she was doing if she wins "The Voice". Without hesitation, she vowed to visit the Philippines.

"I really want to go back and see the beautiful places," revealing she was only three years when she last visited the Philippines. Whenever she joined singing competitions, she would always ask her mom to reward her with a trip to the Philippines. A true Filipina talent with simple wants in life.

27

JENNIFER GARRETT: EPITOME OF A SUCCESFUL FILIPINA

Not all Filipinos in the United States have known her name but Jennifer Garrett, 40 is an epitome of a successful Filipina in the United States and worth emulating. She is an internationally recognized author, business executive and motivational speaker. She has completed seven college degrees: Bachelor of Science (B.S.) Electrical Engineering, B.S. in Biomedical Engineering, Master of Business Administration (M.B.A.), Master of Arts (M.A.) in Communication and Leadership Studies, Juris Doctor (J.D.) Master of Laws (LL.M.) in Business Transactions and LLM in Taxation. She completed her degrees while working and raising five children as a single parent. When asked by Manila Mail what event in her life motivated her to finish seven college degrees, Jennifer was quick to answer that she always had a passion for learning, both in the formal education setting and in life in general.

She strives to learn as much as she can each day. "I do enjoy academia and love pushing myself in that setting. Since I was fortunate to work for companies who had very generous tuition assistance programs and invested in their employees, I decided to pursue a number of college degree programs.

"I also believe that the more knowledge we possess, which doesn't have to come from obtaining degrees, the more valuable of a person we become and can contribute more to society, both inside and outside of the workplace."

Jennifer currently works as an executive coach, corporate consultant, and Judge Advocate for Army National Guard. In addition, she serves on the Board of Counselors for the University of Southern California Marshall's Master of Business Veterans (MBV) program and is an Advisory Board Member for Operation Teammate and is working on an inspirational football film entitles Fourth and Goal which is planned for release in 2019. She is also the author of the book "Move the Ball" and in the process of expanding The Daily Hustle Series, which is a series of booklets that people can utilize to be successful.

     With all her success in life, Jennifer was very proud to give credits to her 74-year-old Filipina mother, Antonia Rubio Garrett, who hails from Meycauayan, Bulacan. "My mother is my role model. When I look at how my mom immigrated to the United States in the 1960's, which was a far-away, unknown and unfamiliar country, I find that truly inspiring. She was the first generation in her family to immigrate to the United States in 1968. She had recently graduated from the University of Santo Tomas in Manila and moved to Chicago, Illinois to pursue a nursing career. Keep that in mind that this was before the internet, e-mail, and smartphones. To give up everything you knew and your family to pursue a career in a completely foreign country, is courageous. My mom only had a few hundred dollars to her name when she moved to Chicago. Through her career, she worked so hard and achieved much success in her field."

As an only child, Jennifer was raised by her parents to value education and always treat people with kindness and respect. When her Dad passed away 2 years ago, Jennifer considered it as the most significant event in her life that shaped the person she is today. "My father died of natural cause not exactly sure what but his unexpected death was a reminder how short life really is and that tomorrow isn't guaranteed for anyone of us. I think about his passing daily and I make sure I live each day purposely, doing things that are important to me and also trying to make as positive of an impact in the lives of others," she explained.

Then came one of the toughest decisions that Jennifer made in her life. She decided to leave her corporate career at Boeing and will be leaving GE in April 2019 to pursue a full-time motivational speaking activities, which was very tough from a financial perspective considering the future of her family as a single mother. Her children are 22 years, 19 years, 15 years, 8 years and 23 months. "I was leaving my guaranteed paycheck behind for an uncertain future and unknown level of income. Like all of us, I had bills to pay and a family to support as a sole-income provider. I say this was a tough decision because of the financial piece, but really this decision was no-brainer.

"My true passion is motivating and inspiring others. When someone tells me 'because of you, I am doing something', you can't put a price tag on that. I was 100% committed to switching career paths and it is something I don't regret. It is important for us to follow our passions in life and not chase a paycheck. I absolutely love sharing inspirational messages to get people excited about reaching their goals," she said.

Jennifer is shining in almost anything in life but she also acknowledged the fact that juggling a career is very challenging for her as single parent. It can be tough working, traveling and raising children but what she focuses on is making sure that has a great relationship with her kids whether its together in person or if it's on a phone call or through texting or Face Timing.

"I travel quite a bit for work and as a working parent who travels often you do miss out on some of your children's moments, sports events and such. While I can't be at every event, what I try to do is be fully present at the activities I am able to partake in. Your children understand work will sometimes take priority." Such are tradeoffs of life when balancing success and family, with grace and agility.

28

CRISTINA OSMEÑA: WALL ST. WHIZ, FILIPINO IMMIGRANT, ERSTWHILE REFUGEE – BUCKS POLITICAL ESTABLISHMENT TO CONTEST CALIFORNIA INCUMBENT IN HOUSE RACE

Despite the large Filipino American presence in California's 14th district – which includes parts of San Francisco and much of San Mateo County, no one from the community has ever run for its seat in the US House of Representatives. That is, not until Cristina Osmeña threw her proverbial hat in the ring.

Osmeña, a scion of the famed Cebu political clan, is running as a Republican in a dark blue congressional district. At 49, the fearless Filipino-American is willing to challenge incumbent Democratic Congresswoman Jackie Speier who was first elected in 2008 (she demolished her Republican rival Angel Cardenas by over 60 percentage points during the 2016 elections).

"It is going to be a challenge as it always is against an incumbent," Ms. Osmeña conceded.

"We are almost two decades apart in age but I don't expect her to remain the incumbent forever," she told the Manila Mail.

She knows it's going to be uphill climb. "What makes it much easier, I suspect is that I am a double minority- a woman of color. I am also an immigrant and a political refugee. The liberal press was getting used to attacking Republicans and their policies for being racist. I am already a minority so that kind of accusation cannot stick with me," she opined.

Ms. Osmeña believes that being a Filipina is one of her strengths and one of the biggest reasons she can run as a Republican. "It may not give me complete immunity, but in a district with a lot of irrational animosity towards Republicans, I think I'm treated with greater tolerance because I am a woman and, importantly, a Filipina.

"I can't recall any times in my career that being a Filipina was a disadvantage. But now I feel that it is an advantage. It's a really nice feeling to step up in crowds and say, 'I am a Filipina,' and feel affirmed just because of that," she declared.

She is the great grand-daughter of former Philippine Pres. Sergio Osmeña (1944-1946) who walked ashore with General Douglas Mac Arthur during the Battle of Leyte Gulf and the daughter of former Philippine Sen. Sergio Osmeña III who escaped a Marcos political prison in 1977.

She is the great grand-daughter of former Philippine Pres. Sergio Osmeña (1944-1946) who walked ashore with General Douglas Mac Arthur during the Battle of Leyte Gulf and the daughter of former Philippine Sen. Sergio Osmeña III who escaped a Marcos political prison in 1977.

She came to the US as a political refugee at the age of six with her mother Maria Angela Barreto Osmeña and brother Sergio Osmeña IV to flee the Martial Law regime of former Philippine President Ferdinand Marcos.

"My father was put in prison three years prior. The three of us moved to the States in an anticipation of an escape he was planning. The first planned escape was foiled. Two years later, in 1977, my father did manage to escape. The US State Department was well aware of his incarceration and gave him political asylum right away. The ease of our acceptance in the United States was facilitated by the late Steve Psinakis," Osmeña recalled, adding in was very painful episode for her family.

She grew up in a Republican neighborhood as a child. When Pres. Ronald Reagan used to visit Los Angeles, she remembered that he would use her high school football field to land his helicopter. "He often stayed at a hotel near my high school. Secondly, I went to Wall Street and this industry leans Republican. I was surrounded by Republican-leaning mentors at an age when my political and economic philosophy was being shaped. Ultimately, I am fiscally aligned with the Republicans. While this is not the issue that makes the headlines (fiscal responsibility is not very controversial), it is my defining issue," she explained.

With a Bachelor of Arts in English from University of California Berkeley, she settled into a 20-year career in the financial industry working in banking and investment management. She was an equity analyst when the World Trade Center in New York City was attacked on September 11, 2001.

She held an executive role in the solar industry and in 2017 became the Vice President for Corporate Development of SunPreme, a solar module manufacturer based in Sunnyvale, Ca. before leaving to focus on her candidacy as a congresswoman.

She is married to Stephen O'Rourke, co-founder of a firm that develops large scale renewable energy power plants. O'Rourke is a graduate of the United States Naval Academy and a veteran of the first Gulf War, stationed as an officer on the U.S.S Simon Bolivar, a ballistic missile submarine.

In 2004, she was named one of the three Best on The Street Analysts by the Wall Street Journal for stock picking and she writes a column for the Philippine News.

What motivated Ms. Osmeña to run for public office was the urging of her mentor, businessman Gerald Gold. "He first brought up the idea a long time ago. He passed away two years ago at the age of 84. When he first mentioned it, I did not take the idea seriously. But when he died in 2016 and the public rhetoric around immigrants started getting contentious, I spoke with other people about this idea and this got the process started," she said.

Her uncle, Cebu City Mayor Tommy Osmeña is the most influential Filipino politician in her life. "I have seen him in action up close and have been exposed to the kitchen cabinet meetings in his early campaigns. I must have picked up some of his methodology in the course of this experiences. Nevertheless, I was very careful not to consult with him before my candidacy became public. I only announced it to him when the news started to leak," she explained.

She didn't ask any advice from her father Sergio III when she decided to run and was very careful not to consult any family member involved in politics. "Not being in touch with my father is an important point. I was very sensitive to the fact that this is an American election and should not be influenced by anyone in a foreign government. I did consult with my mother as I went through the decision process. My mother is an American citizen and lives in the Bay Area."

There are however some issues that her party might find running against the Republican orthodoxy. As a Filipino immigrant and political refugee, for instance, she is openly supportive of DACA although she opposes so-called sanctuary states.

"I think a country has the right to control who crosses in and out of its borders. I am supportive of a Dream Act. I am similar to a Dreamer though I was not illegal, I grew up here under political asylum, became very American and yet was not a citizen. I understand how that feels. Children who immigrated illegally cannot be held to the same kind of accountability as adults.

"Law-abiding Dreamers should get a path to citizenship. I am against sanctuary states. I don't see anything productive in instructing one branch of law enforcement (local) to not cooperate with another (federal). It contributes to the inefficiency of our government and consumes more tax dollars," she explained.

Ms. Osmeña acknowledged that she is a moderate Republican when it comes to social issues but fiscally conservative. When asked to cite where she agrees with or disagrees with President Trump, she stated: "I really like the new tax law that was passed last year. It encourages entrepreneurship and eliminates some complexity. I agree with Trump on his caution towards China. I think China is already a formidable economic adversary.

"I don't agree with his nationalistic approach to the rest of world trade. The benefits of comparative advantage have already been proven. Aside from that, the US benefits when the world uses our dollars to trade.

"I am mixed on immigration. I think the US should have more secure borders. Having people illegally cross our borders means we can't even account for who is in our country. Of course, that is a security issue. However, I think quotas on legal immigration should go up, not down. I think legal immigrants are generally beneficial to our economy," she averred.

Cristina Osmeña, erstwhile immigrant, understands the allure of America, the value of its foreign born, and what that experience can bring to the power of public service.

29

PINOY'S TRUMP- INSPIRED GOWN MEANT TO COUNTER 'HATERS'

Hollywood singer-songwriter Joy Villa generated some buzz and controversy on the red carpet of this year's Grammy Awards by donning the "Make America Great Again" gown – the creation of Filipino immigrant fashion designer, Andre Soriano. I met Joy and Andre at a Trump rally in Washington D.C. last March 4. Andre and I had been exchanging text messages and talking on the phone about a guesting for my radio program *"Pilipinas Sa Amerika."*

The Filipino-American Journey

Andre was born in Paranaque, Manila. He explained that Joy was not only a client but also a close friend. With their hugs, their mutual respect was obvious. They also share an affinity with Pres. Trump, insisting he's all about love, peace, unity, and not the kind negativity often depicted in media.

"There are a lot of celebrities who want to hurt the President," he explains. He confessed he was inspired to create the "Make America Great Again" gown after hearing Madonna's profanity-laced tirade during the Women's March in Washington.

"I heard Madonna say she wanted to bomb the White House. I'm a proud Filipino-American and my mother brought me and my three siblings here in the United States when I was 15 to have a better future. I love the American Dream, and this country is so powerful and there are so many privileges and opportunities for everyone," he said.

"There is only one President in the US right now and that is President Trump and not Hillary Clinton. I told Joy, I really have a design for you however I'm changing it because there is so much hatred and hostility from Hollywood celebrities," he declared.

"We have to make a statement on what is right for our country, of what we believe in, for the Constitution. I have a gown for you," Soriano recounted.

"It's going to be a Trump's dress," he told Joy and checked if she voted for Trump. After affirming their political loyalties, he set out to build the "statement dress" he had in mind. "Her music is about static so I decided to create static for the Grammys."

"After Joy agreed with my suggestion, I went to my front porch *kinuha ko 'yong bandila n*i Trump for his campaign to blend it out, piece it out and make it a gown in four days," Andre revealed. Still, Andre is not one to ram his politics. As a Filipino immigrant though he believes the best way to express himself and his passions is through the fashion designs he creates. He believes that everyone should respect each other and avoid inciting violence or hatred.

He's lived with husband Thomas Brown, a former building contractor, for last two decades. Brown is 70 and Andre is 46 years old but he says they have a peaceful life. He said they live the "American Dream" day to day, unmindful of a person's race or sexual orientation. All human beings, Andre believes, have a responsibility to promote what love and unity is all about.

"We are all children of God and I believe that we should love each other. We only live on this planet once and why not have a better world rather than hating each other."

Andre, grew up in a family who liked to dress up but is also very religious, conservative and middle class. Raised in the Philippines, he credits his mom for instilling confidence in him by accepting the fact that he and his older brother are both gays.

"She accepted our sexual preferences and she would tell us to follow our dreams and hearts, always do good things to people and never think that because some people have money they are better than you. Everyone is equal according to my Mom."

As an immigrant, Andre also had his challenges: he flipped burgers for McDonalds and worked as a lobby receptionist at United Airlines earning $7 an hour.

Andre, attended school at Fashion Institute of Design and Merchandising in San Francisco, Ca. In 2004, he started his fashion business selling active- and ready-to-wear clothes. His career took off when Rihanna discovered him in 2013 and invited him to join her reality show "Styled to Rock."

His work has been featured in many fashion magazines including New York Fashion Times, Vanity Fair, Apparel News, etc. His designs have been worn by celebrities like Macy Gray, Courtney Love, Jessica Sanchez and Bai Ling.

He wants to create another "statement gown" for possibly First Lady Melania Trump and First Daughters Ivanka and Tiffany Trump. Seems like an obvious, natural fit between designer and First Family that may well happen.

30
CATCHING A GLIMPSE OF CHAOTIC WORLD OF POLITICS

The Filipino-American Journey

The excitement and glamour of national politics can sometimes prove irresistible for the young, especially those expecting civility and logic to rule in crafting the people's work. Louie Tan Vital, 22, of Seattle, WA. finished last a four-month internship at the United States Congress last Aug. 18; what she got was a sobering glimpse into the chaotic world of American politics.

Being a congressional intern is not an easy job. It has all the emotional and physical stress of politics, which she did not expect. In the office where she worked, she was the first person to answer the phones, check emails, postal mails. The legislative staff usually works on policy and research but Vital's job was focused mostly on constituent correspondence.

"When hundreds of people call or write in, I aggregate and transmit the constituent's concerns to the legislative assistants. Because I'm on the frontlines, I receive the raw emotions, the breaks in their voices that communicate fear, hope and joy," she explained. "It's difficult to disassociate myself from it when these emotions are painfully real and humanizing. I feel their emotions just as deeply as they do, the hard part is collecting and absorbing their pain," she added.

The pressure was too much for her. After only a month of working at the U.S. Congress, Vital broke down as a congressional intern and decided to write down her emotions on her Facebook account. Her Facebook post received 46,000 likes and more than 8,000 comments.

"I broke down in Congress slumped against the hallway. My sobs bouncing off the ceiling. Is this business as usual? Working for Congress is like always being in crisis mode. 9:00 am latest terrorist attacks, 9:02 am internalize abuses on the phone, 9:06 am sound robotically pleasant with tears fresh on my face. "Hi there, thank you for calling the office of Congressman.""

"Crouched in the hallway, sobbing into my pencil skirt, absorbing every racial slur into the lines in my forehead, Yes! I have gray hairs at 22, I'm forgetting how to eat, sleep or relax. Constituents from around the country call every day to share their hopes, fears, and anger," she wrote in anguish.

"It's beautiful and painful and I can't help but absorb every word. Yesterday, I sorted through a barrage of racist hate mail; people have said unspeakable things to me, thinking I'm not a person of color. I am the only Filipino I know in the United States House of Representatives, but I'm looking for the day when I won't be."

Vital recalled that she was tired, mad, embarrassed that she couldn't keep herself together that day. She said that her breakdown also began a beautiful journey of self -reflection and inner strength. She knew that moment that she was part of something greater. Meanwhile, Louie Tan Vital also experienced the intimidation just because of her Asian race. There had been times when she walks into a room and she's the only woman and the only person in color. It is often the case that she is the only Asian woman.

The rough and abrasive world of politics has not forced her to shy away from her interest in government. Now that her internship ended, Vital will begin to pursue her graduate studies at the University of Washington's Evans School of Public Policy and Governance for her Master's in Public Administration to focus and learn more about domestic social policy and international development.

When Manila Mail asked Vital if she wants to be a politician. Vital explained that the word politician has such a negative connotation to it. "I would say I aspire to be a public servant. To clarify I do want to become an elected official so I can represent my community in ways I feel like we are not being served.

"With the population of Asian Pacific Islanders in America expected to double in the upcoming generation, it is absolutely critical to have people that look like us in power. If members of our own community are not present politically, that means people from other communities will be making decisions about us, and for us. That will have dangerous repercussions for our children. I want to represent our Filipino community with pride and lead other Filipinos into the political realm."

With determination, she looks to her next political challenge. "My parents did not immigrate here for me to be shy or be scared in this room with the political elite. They came here so I can make this place my own, so I will." She knows the world of politics will not change, so she must change, armed with more education and emotional strength if she's to succeed in that world.

31

FIL-AM'S LIFELONG SEARCH FOR BIOLOGICAL PARENTS ENDS WITH HELP OF SOCIAL MEDIA

Growing up in an African-American family as the first adopted child, Alexis Danielle Brown Windsor, 35, of Clinton, Md. wondered about her identity, hoping that one day she would be able to find her biological parents in the Philippines.

Alexis was given up for adoption when she was eight weeks old and was adopted by military couple "Mr. and Mrs. Brown" stationed at Clark Air Force Base in the Philippines during the 1980's.

Mr. Brown was a navigator aboard a C-130 cargo plane and his wife was a secretary for the military. Alexis found out about her adoption when she was 6 years old. She has another adopted brother from Little Rock, Arkansas who is an African-American.

"I have always felt a sense of emptiness and void in my life. While I appreciate the life I was given here by my adoptive parents, I longed to know where I came from and who I am. I never felt complete or part of anyone," she lamented.

"My younger brother was always around with his culture, my parents are black, my brother is black. He never felt out of place. Everything was normal for him. I looked different and I got bullied as I was growing up," Alexis added. Alexis was born August 9, 1982 in Marisol Village, Angeles City, Pampanga as Ofelia Pamindanan Belmonte. She was the 7th child of Josefina Belmonte, a household help in Pampanga and Diosdado Belmonte of Bicol who was a wood carver, now working as a driver in Metro Manila.

Josefina became very sick after giving birth to Ofelia. She decided to send her children including Ofelia to an orphanage in Angeles City hoping that the siblings will be taking care of and will get them back after she recovers from sickness. However, circumstances created an opportunity when a certain Marta Torres met the Brown couple when Ofelia was two months old. She told them that there was a baby in the orphanage that was abandoned and had no identity or name. Before her 2nd birthday, Ofelia was legally adopted as Alexis Danielle Brown.

The Belmonte family met with the Browns about Ofelia's adoption. It was something that they didn't really want to do at the time. Burdened by poverty they prayed and hoped that Ofelia would be in good hands and have a better future in America with her adoptive parents. Alexis was brought up by the Browns with a lot of discipline and work ethic. She was raised to have a military mentality and was sent to a military school during her teenage days. "I was teased and bullied most of the time for being an Asian. I was a rebel when I was a teenager. I always feel like an outcast. I didn't have a father-daughter relationship. I didn't get along with my Dad and I wanted to find my real parents," Alexis explained.

When her teenage years were over, Alexis tried to build a decent relationship with her adoptive parents and studied graphic design at the University of Maryland. She now works at the Federal Aviation Administration with her husband, Andre Windsor Sr. They have two kids Brianna, 13 and Andre Windsor Jr. who is seven years old.

On May 22, 2017 a week after Mother's Day, Alexis finally found her long-lost family in the Philippines. A Filipino friend put her in contact with John Guerrera who is the administrator for a Faeebook group "The Amerasian Children Looking For Their American Gl Fathers." Guerrera was able to track the Belmonte family in Angeles City, Pampanga and connected Alexis to them after both parties verified everything.

"People were helping me left and right. Strangers knowing my social worker and knowing people with my family name, Belmonte. And in less than 24 hours I was able to be put in touch with my niece, nephew and sisters. The next thing you know I am video chatting for over an hour with my mom and siblings. I learned both my mom, dad and siblings are alive and I have six brothers, four sisters and 35 nieces and nephews. "We cried, we laughed, we smiled and most of all bonded like I've never done before. The empty hole in my heart is filled. I felt so much love. I can't wait to go to the Philippines and meet my whole family," Alexis enthused.

One of the hardest things for Alexis was to tell her adoptive parents that she found her birth parents. "I didn't want them to feel like I love them any less or think I wasn't grateful for the good life they have afforded to give me and I wanted to share my joy and excitement," she explained. It may not be easy for her adoptive parents to accept the fact that Alexis finally found her birth parents; but Alexis now feels complete as a person and her kids are embracing every moment, she spends with two sets of parents. For her, Facebook became a way to complete the circle of her identity and bring closure to the mystery of a life left behind in the Philippines.

32

THE MATH OF MIGRATING TO AMERICA

Numbers can add or subtract, but for my high school math teacher, Romerico "Mikoy" Jamora, 54, and his family, they added to his life in ways he never envisioned before coming to America. Christmas is usually the happiest time for Filipinos in the US. During Christmas 2004, Mr. Jamora was alone, away from his family for the second time. First in Japan, then in the U.S. It wasn't as bad as he thought at the time because he was traveling across the US with friends during vacations and breaks. On that first Christmas, he made it to Disneyland – the happiest place on earth, as they say. But his family's journey to America was not easy.

Born in Tina, Badiangan, Iloilo, Jamora grew up very poor, raised in a farm by a single mom who could barely make both ends meet. Although his father came from a prominent family, he never acknowledged his son as he had another family. "When I was nine, I remember going with my mom to his big house, a mansion, to meet him," Jamora recalls, "but we never had a chance because we were told to leave. That was the last time we tried to contact him."

Poverty almost forced him to quit school. Instead, it challenged him to strive harder. He graduated high school valedictorian, with top awards and honors. He was also offered a scholarships and financial assistance from Balikbayan residents of Tina, notably the families of Alfredo Galez and Lucas Estante. At the West Visayas State University in Iloilo City, Jamora supported himself doing house painting and carpentry. His mother's meagre earnings as a house maid also helped.

During his years teaching math at Iloilo National High School, he rose from the ranks of being a regular teacher to becoming Department Head, Regional Mathematics Supervisor at DepEd Region VI and later Mathematics Coordinator at the DepEd Division of Iloilo. He won several nationwide honors, including the prestigious Dr. Juan Salcedo Jr. Science Award. His rewards included being sent to Australia, Japan and Malaysia to train on technology and cooperative learning.

In 2004, he saw math as a passport to a new life when he applied for a Visiting International Faculty program in the U.S. But the immigration process was a long and draining struggle, financially and emotionally.

"We spent a lot of money just to have our papers fixed from a visiting J1 to a working H1-B," he explains. "My wife had to change her visa from J2 dependent to H2 dependent still and to H1-B working visa. Our employer had to file a sponsorship to grant our green card and we waited for another five years to file our citizenship." They finally got their green cards on June 2013, after a long and disheartening wait.

Jamora's wife, Maria Luz Cantara, 52, is also a math teacher from Leon, Iloilo and a Cum Laude graduate from the same university Jamora attended. Upon arriving in North Carolina, she worked at McDonald's. She and her husband are now math teachers at Maury High School in Norfolk, Virginia.

Having achieved some measure of economic stability, the Jamoras are proud of their children's accomplishments as well. Their 27-year-old daughter, Mary Daphne graduated her Bachelor of Arts, Summa Cum Laude at Old Dominion University, Norfolk, Virginia in 2012 and got a perfect score in the Praxis (Teacher's Exam). She now works as a Kindergarten teacher in Magdeburg, Germany, where she married Carlsten Neubert, a German citizen. Their son, 24-year-old Von graduated his Associate Degree in Engineering Summa Cum Laude at Tidewater Community College and Magna Cum Laude in his Engineering Degree at Old Dominion University, Norfolk, Virginia last May 2018. He now pursues his master's degree in the same university with full scholarship and stipend doing research work for NASA. Their youngest daughter, 12-year-old Aimee Erikah, is in middle school and has been a consistent honor student since her elementary grades.

"The accomplishments of my children will be attached to their names wherever they go and whatever they do in life," Jamora exudes with pride. "Where I am today, I attribute to my perseverance and hard work. Poverty spurred my determination to succeed because I don't want to stay where I began throughout my life."

The math of migrating to America added up for Jamora and his family. They hope for no divisions or subtractions in their future, only to multiply their family and add their small part to the exponential, positive future of America. To honor their adopted country, Jamora coined their youngest daughter's name after America.

Acknowledgment

It's a great honor and privilege to be able to hear and write the stories of Filipinos in the United States. Their life experiences, struggles and success stories are thought provoking and will always be an inspiration. Journalism is my passion in life and my civic duty that I could not just leave behind when I left the Philippines in 2002.

My special thanks to *Manila Mail* newspaper, especially to **Attorney Januario "Warie" Azarcon** for allowing me to put into a book the articles that I wrote for the newspaper. I will always be grateful to Attorney Warie for his sage guidance and for giving me the opportunity to develop my skills in writing and to be a part of *Manila Mail*. To **Rodney Jaleco**, Manila Mail's Associate Editor and **Jon Melegrito**, Editor-in-Chief, together your collegial and talented editorial skills greatly empowered and enabled my writing. I appreciate your combined help to come up with a collection of great and inspiring articles.

Many thanks to all my colleagues and friends in *Manila Mail*. Thank you for treating me with kindness and love. To my **RMN ILOILO** family, especially to station manager **Ronel Sorbito**, thank you for your unwavering support and for giving me the opportunity to broadcast from America to the Philippines and to my co-hosts on the radio show *"Pilipinas sa Amerika"* **Joel Franco, Magie Maleriado and the RMN ILOILO technicians.**

Many thanks to **Mike Seneriches** for giving me the idea for the book title; to **Emmanuel Mejorada Welsh** for developing a beautiful front and back cover of the book; to **Eunice Barbara Novio** and **Anthony Esguerra** who are always ready to help me with my news sources. To **Tatay Jobo Elizes**, my publisher, many thanks for all your assistance and critical help.

And to all my friends and families in the Philippines and United States, thank you all for believing in me that I can make a difference in the lives of others by committing myself to journalism and community service. To the people that I interviewed thank you for trusting me with the story of your life experiences, struggles and successes.

And lastly to my loving husband **Barry,** my everyday inspiration and source of strength. Thank you for encouraging me to be the best that I can be. I wouldn't be able to accomplish everything that I wanted and hoped for in my life without your presence, support, love and guidance.

Made in USA - Kendallville, IN
1029896_9781726724975
12.06.2019 1040